IMMIGRANT ROOTS

Captivating Stories that will Activate Your Abundance to Reach the Top 1% of Wealth in the USA

GUILLERMO CHÁVEZ-ANGELES

IMMIGRANT ROOTS

This book is a compilation of stories from numerous people who have each contributed a chapter and is designed to provide inspiration to our readers.

It is sold with the understanding that the publisher and the individual authors are not engaged in the rendering of psychological, legal, accounting or other professional advice. The content and views in each chapter are the sole expression and opinion of its author and not necessarily the views of Fig Factor Media, LLC.

For more information, contact:
Fig Factor Media, LLC | www.figfactormedia.com
Immigrant Roots | www.angelesbooks.com

Cover Design by DG Marco Alvarez
Layout by LDG Juan Manuel Serna Rosales

FIG FACTOR MEDIA

Printed in the United States of America

ISBN: 9-78-1-961600-6-07
Library of Congress Control Number: 2025906135

DEDICATION

To Alexa & Brielle,

You are my why, the driving force behind everything I do. A part of my being, my purpose, and my greatest motivation.

May this book serve as an inspiration to you and to every reader who comes across it. May the stories within these pages remind you that no dream is too big, no goal is out of reach, and that our journeys—rooted in resilience, culture, and ambition—are meant to inspire greatness.

Always chase your dreams, and build your success on passion, resilience, and the belief that anything is possible.

With all my love,

Your Dad

TABLE OF CONTENTS

ACKNOWLEDGEMENTS

First and foremost, I give my deepest gratitude to our Superior Being—whom I know as God and who lives at the core center of my being. You are my guide and my strength. Thank You for Your endless blessings, for the wisdom to walk this path, and for the purpose You have placed in me.

To my parents and to the parents of countless other immigrants: your courage and sacrifice are the foundation of everything we do. Leaving behind your home, your family, and everything familiar to give your children a better future is an act of love that can never be repaid. This book is a tribute to your resilience and the legacy you built through your hard work and sacrifice.

To the nine incredible authors who have joined me on this journey—not just as collaborators, but as friends—I appreciate each of you. Our paths crossed for a reason, and it's an honor to do this together. You were chosen because I admire your dedication and character. Let us continue growing, striving to become the best versions of ourselves, paying it forward in our communities, and uplifting those around us.

To all the people who have supported me throughout my career—you are the reason this book is possible today. Not only did you believe in me as a new entrepreneur and business owner, but you also supported something much bigger. *Immigrant Roots* is more than just a book; it is a movement designed to bring motivation, unity, and a resource to inspire the next generation of entrepreneurs. Your unwavering encouragement and trust have fueled this vision, and for that, I am forever grateful.

With gratitude,
Guillermo Chávez-Angeles

FOREWORD
By Vicente Del Real

In a moment of history where adversity and negative rhetoric often seek to silence the voices and stories of immigrants, *Immigrant Roots* stands as a powerful testament to those who dare to dream beyond their circumstances. Grounded in the immigrant experience and forged through resilience, these stories not only acknowledge the struggle of arriving in a new land but also celebrate the strength, faith, and community that emerge from it. This book not only narrates personal hardships but also explores how obstacles can become opportunities, and how those opportunities can become a path for transformation. Through these stories, we see how challenges ignite growth, shaping individuals who not only overcome but also inspire us to do the same. My hope is that you, as a reader, are not only challenged but inspired to see the obstacles in your personal story as stepping stones.

The journeys chronicled within these pages will help you reflect on your own personal story, and how many chapters of our own stories do not unfold as we hope. However, we all can learn from our mistakes and find purpose in the most challenging times. These ten stories in *Immigrant Roots* reflect the diverse and powerful experiences of immigrants who, in the face of many challenges, found strength in faith and community. Each story captures a unique path—from uncertainty to ownership, from isolation to community, from suffering to sacrifice—serving as a reminder that our stories may not be perfect, but that is what makes them special.

The stories of immigrants must be told because they illuminate the human experience in profound ways. These narratives shed light on the courage, resilience, and sacrifices that define the immigrant journey. By sharing these stories, we not only honor the struggles and triumphs of those who have crossed borders in search of a better life but also challenge stereotypes and foster empathy. These voices serve as powerful reminders of the strength that diversity brings to our communities and the invaluable contributions immigrants make to society a better place.

In a time when negative rhetoric surrounding immigrants often dominates public discourse, *Immigrant Roots* serves as a powerful counter-narrative. By highlighting the profound contributions immigrants make to society, this book challenges misconceptions and uplifts the voices that are too often unheard. These stories are not just about overcoming adversity but about enriching communities, driving innovation, and strengthening the social fabric that binds us all.

As you turn these pages, you will encounter stories of personal battles and breakthroughs, of faith that moves mountains, but most importantly a story that any immigrant or descent of immigrants can read and relate to. These stories serve as a reminder that true leadership is born from compassion, and that the pursuit of your dreams requires both courage and humility.

May this book not only inspire you, but also remind you of the power of your own story and the importance of sharing this treasure with others, for the common good, as we walk together toward building a more just and compassionate world.

With deep respect and admiration,
Vicente Del Real
Founder & CEO
Iskali

INTRODUCTION

Immigrant Roots: *A Movement for Change*

This book is more than a collection of stories—it is a movement. A movement to change the narrative within our cultures, where too often we pull each other down instead of lifting each other up. It is time to break that cycle. It is time to be the change.

For too long, immigrant stories have been told through the lens of struggle alone, rather than resilience, innovation, and success. This book is about rewriting that narrative. It is about shifting the mindset within our own communities—choosing collaboration over competition, mentorship over isolation, and empowerment over doubt. It is a movement for change, one that ensures the next generation of immigrant entrepreneurs and leaders see not just obstacles, but opportunities.

Through mentorship, collaboration, and paying it forward, we can empower the next generation of immigrant entrepreneurs and leaders. We can show America—the land of opportunity—that immigrants are not just contributors to the economy; we are innovators, creators, and builders of a stronger future.

In *Immigrant Roots,* you will find ten powerful

stories of resilience, each one a testament to the unbreakable spirit of those who dared to dream beyond their circumstances. Each of these authors—Estefania, Tammy, Laura, Pablo, Elia, Antonio, Nancy, Teresa, Alix, and Guillermo—has faced defining moments that tested their strength and shaped their journey.

For Estefania, that moment came when the opportunity arose to purchase a bankrupt construction business—an industry not typically known for having female owners. Rebuilding it wasn't just about saving a company; it was about proving to herself that she could take control of her destiny, break cycles of struggle, and redefine what was possible—not just for herself, but for every woman who has ever been told she doesn't belong in the room. That decision didn't just shape her; it made her the leader, entrepreneur, and advocate she is today.

For Tammy, her defining moment came when she found alignment in the three most important relationships in life—her faith, herself, and her spouse. Once she had these in order, everything changed for the better—not just for her, but for her children, her relationship with her mother, her success at work, and her influence on others. That clarity became the foundation for the life and legacy she is building today.

For Alix, that moment came when he had to overcome self-doubt and push past the mental barriers that stood between him and his dream of becoming a doctor. His journey wasn't just about academic challenges; it was about proving to himself that he was capable, that he belonged, and that he could achieve what once seemed impossible.

For Teresa, resilience was born from devastation. When her business burned to the ground, leaving her with nothing and no safety net, she faced a choice—stay defeated or rise stronger. "From the ashes, I rose like a phoenix, turning loss into strength and darkness into light." With unwavering determination, she rebuilt, proving that even in our lowest moments we have the power to reclaim our future and emerge stronger than before.

For Laura, her defining moment came not long ago when she lost the pillars of her family—her parents and her brother. Losing her father made her realize she wasn't as strong as she once believed. Losing her mother taught her that any plans made with loved ones must be acted on before it's too late. And losing her brother made her understand that the things we often complain about are insignificant compared to the pain of losing someone we love. Through it all, she has surrendered to the will of

God, accepting that life unfolds according to His plan, not hers.

For Elia, resilience meant finding the courage to leave an unhappy marriage and become a single mother, defying cultural expectations and redefining what it meant to stand on her own. Her inspiring decisions led her to create a legacy for her daughter and grandchildren. Not only is this admirable but it's something that she can be proud of and know her resilience led her to success.

For Pablo, transformation came when he stopped seeing himself as a victim and overcame the "poor me" mentality. He realized that his circumstances did not define him—that he had the power to change his story. By shifting his mindset, he took control of his life and turned obstacles into opportunities, proving that resilience begins with perspective.

For Nancy, her defining moment came when her brother helped her put things into perspective. She had hesitated about pursuing law school, worried about her age, but he reminded her that time should never dictate our choices. "You will be thirty eventually anyway, so you'll be thirty and be an attorney, or you'll be thirty and still be the assistant to the attorney," he told her. That realization changed everything. She understood then that it's never too late to become who we are meant to be, and she chose to take control of her future.

For Antonio, resilience wasn't just about overcoming a kidney transplant and other health challenges at a young age—it was about using those struggles to shape the man he would become. His experiences built not only his strength but also his deep compassion, teaching him that everyone is fighting their own battles. Instead of holding him back, his hardships became the driving force behind his perseverance and empathy.

And finally, for Guillermo, the ultimate test came when he had to make the painful decision to file for bankruptcy after previously achieving great success in his career. Hitting rock bottom tested him in every way—his confidence, his beliefs, and his resilience. But through that hardship, he learned two of life's most important lessons: material success comes and goes, and failure is not the end but a new beginning. From rock bottom, there is only one way to go—up. And with that realization, he rebuilt, stronger and wiser than before.

Life will continue to present defining moments—challenges, opportunities, and turning points that shape who we are and who we become. It is crucial to recognize these moments, to pay attention, and to be willing to shift direction if necessary. Growth requires adaptability, and sometimes, the path you started on is not the one meant for you. The ability to embrace change and move forward with courage is what truly defines resilience.

Never stop learning, never stop growing, and always continue to push yourself to new heights. Success is not just about talent or luck—it is about perseverance, belief, and the willingness to rise, again and again, despite the odds.

This is our moment to rewrite the narrative. To support, uplift, and inspire. To pay it forward so that those who come after us will find not only opportunity but a community that believes in their success.

Let's be the change.

AUTHOR CHAPTER STORIES

A STORY OF RESILIENCE

GUILLERMO CHAVEZ-ANGELES

"Through all the struggles, the hardships, and the uncertainty, I've learned that the best things in life often come when you least expect them."

MY ROOTS

I was born in Guadalajara, Jalisco, Mexico, the second youngest of four children. My childhood was filled with simplicity and the warmth of family, growing up in a country where tradition and community played a big role. We lived a modest life, but we were very happy. I had no sense of how much my life would change as I grew older.

In 1995, our family life took a curve ball. Mexico's economy collapsed, and my father lost all three of his jobs. We watched as our stable life unraveled. Struggling to provide for us, my father made the difficult decision to leave for Chicago, hoping to find better opportunities. His departure was hard to understand at the time. I was only 12 years old to grasp the weight of his decision, but the absence left an emptiness in our home.

Soon after, my mother followed him, leaving my three sisters and me by ourselves. We were just kids—aged 8, 12, 16, and 20—trying to survive without parental guidance. We had no one to turn to, no family support. It felt like we were completely alone in a world that was unfamiliar and unforgiving.

At 12 years old, I was left to take on responsibilities far beyond my years. My older sisters did their best to keep the family together, but we were all just children, trying to find our way. We had to grow up fast. We learned to cook, clean, and manage a household on our own. We were forced to take on the role of parents, even though we were just kids ourselves.

The loneliness was overwhelming at times. I missed my parents desperately and often wondered when they would return. But we adapted. We relied on each other, our bond as siblings grew stronger with every passing day. We learned to survive, to make do with what little we had, and to carry the weight of our circumstances.

CROSSING BORDERS, BREAKING BARRIERS

In 1999 we reunited with our parents in Evanston, a north suburb of Chicago. It was supposed to be a new beginning. A chance to start fresh in a country full of opportunity. But reality quickly set in. I was sixteen, an undocumented teenager, and I didn't speak a word of English.

I was enrolled in ESL classes, and every day felt like a battle. I struggled to communicate, to make sense of the new world around me. The language barrier was frustrating, and I often felt isolated and out of place. I wanted to go back to Mexico, back to the only life I knew, but I couldn't. I had no choice but to push through. I spent my days trying to understand my lessons, my classmates, and the culture. I was homesick, but I also had a fire inside of me. I knew I had to learn, adapt, and make this new life work for me.

After high school, I decided to follow in my older

sister's footsteps and enter the real estate business. It was 2001, and the housing market was thriving. I started working as a loan consultant doing mortgage loans, learning the ropes of the business. Over the next few years, I found success and began to build a life I was proud of.

LIFE'S CURVEBALL

Life has a way of throwing unexpected challenges, and at 21 I was hit with one of the toughest battles of my life. What started as a seemingly harmless infection, initially diagnosed as a spider bite, turned into a long and painful journey for answers. The symptoms persisted, and I found myself going from hospital to hospital, desperately searching for a diagnosis.

I finally made the decision to visit the Mayo Clinic, hoping for some clarity. After countless tests and consultations, I was diagnosed with WHIM syndrome, a rare immune disorder. It was a moment that changed everything. I was later referred to the National Institutes of Health (NIH), where I began receiving specialized treatment.

Receiving this diagnosis felt like a heavy blow. I was young and just starting to build my life, and now I was faced with a chronic health condition. I had two choices:

I could feel sorry for myself, even consider applying for disability as many others with my condition had done, or I could choose to move forward, continue to dream big, and work hard towards my goals.

I chose the latter. I refused to let this diagnosis define me or dictate my future. Instead, I used it as motivation to push through, to become stronger and more resilient. This experience taught me that life will always find a way to throw you curveballs, and it's up to us to change the trajectory or grow from it.

A NEW BEGINNING

In the midst of the hustle, life threw a blessing my way. I married my wife, and that gave me hope. My legal status changed, and I became a legal resident of the United States. This was a turning point—an opportunity I would forever be grateful for. It opened the door for me to fully embrace the American Dream, to build a future for myself and my family. allowing me to fully step into my potential and embrace everything I had worked for.

By my early twenties, I had several rental properties and my own home in downtown Chicago. I felt like I was living the American Dream. I had worked hard to get there, and everything seemed to be falling into place. I had a stable income, my own place, and a growing sense of pride in what I had accomplished. But the good times didn't last long. In 2007, the housing market crashed. The economy plummeted, and the financial world crumbled. What had seemed like a solid foundation turned out to be a fragile house of cards.

ROCK BOTTOM AND REVELATION

The crash of 2007 was devastating. The housing market collapsed, and with it, my entire financial world. The properties I had worked so hard to acquire became liabilities. My income dried up, and my debts piled up. It was as if everything I had built had vanished overnight.

In an attempt to protect my credit and salvage what little I had left; I drained my savings. From 2007 to 2009, I spent every dollar I had to keep afloat, but eventually, I had no choice but to file for bankruptcy in 2009.

Losing everything was a blow I never saw coming. I had thought I was successful. I thought I had everything under control. But in an instant, it was all gone. The future I had built for myself had crumbled to dust. Filing for bankruptcy was a hard pill to swallow. I had worked so hard to build something, and now it felt like it had all been for nothing. I was left with nothing but debts and regrets. But in the midst of all this despair, I received news that would change my life forever: I was going to be a father.

At first, I was overwhelmed. I had just lost everything. How could I provide for my child when I could barely take care of myself? The fear of failure crept in. The uncertainty of my future weighed heavily on my shoulders. But I refused to give up. I knew I had to find a way to make things right. I wasn't going to let my child grow up in the same conditions I had. I began searching for my big break, for an opportunity to start over.

THE HUSTLE FOR HOPE

I took on every job I could find. I sold life insurance, organic products, and got involved in multi-level marketing. I did phone sales and any other job that promised some kind of income. Nothing seemed to stick, but I kept pushing forward. I knew that if I kept working, eventually something would give.

From 2009 to 2014, I hustled relentlessly. There were days when I felt like I was running in circles, but I refused to give up. I knew that every job I took, every lesson I learned, was preparing me for the right opportunity.

In 2014, I finally crossed paths with a recruiter who introduced me to the State Farm agent program. The idea of becoming my own business owner was something I had always dreamed of, but I never thought it was possible. It felt like a sign from God.

Looking back, I realized that all the jobs I had done in the years since the crash had prepared me for this moment. The licenses I had obtained, the sales experience I had gained—everything had led me here. I didn't have to start from scratch. I had the tools I needed to succeed.

Starting my own business wasn't easy. There were moments of doubt, times when I wondered if I was making the right decision. But I knew I had no other choice. I had to take the leap.

THE GIFT OF ADOPTION

In 2020, during the global pandemic, our family received another blessing: the gift of adoption. My wife and I welcomed our second daughter into our lives. This gift, during such a challenging time, reminded me that even in the darkest moments, miracles can happen.

The birth of my second daughter was a reminder that life continues, even in the face of adversity. Through all the struggles, the hardships, and the uncertainty, I've learned that the best things in life often come when you least expect them.

PURPOSE THROUGH PAIN

For anyone reading this and dreaming of becoming an entrepreneur, let me tell you: sometimes, during the hardest times, we don't understand why it's happening to us. We don't see the purpose behind the struggle. But there is always a reason. Every hardship, every failure, is shaping us into the people we are meant to be.

For me, those six years of hardship and searching for my big break were not in vain. They prepared me for the opportunity that would change everything. The struggles, the failures, and the setbacks—they were all part of the journey.

This isn't just my story. It's a story of perseverance and resilience. It's proof that no matter how hard things get, you can overcome them.

TIPS FOR WEALTH & SUCCESS

1. **Seek Mentors Early On**

   Don't wait to find guidance—start seeking mentors as early as middle school or high school. Learning from those who've walked the path before you can open doors, provide insights, and help you avoid costly mistakes. The sooner you start, the stronger your foundation will be.

2. **Develop an Addiction for Growth**

   Wealth and success require a relentless commitment

to learning and self-improvement. Develop an obsession with personal growth and business acumen. The more you invest in yourself, the more opportunities you'll create.

3. **Embrace Spirituality and a Higher Purpose**
   Stay grounded in your spirituality and connect with a purpose greater than yourself. When you have a reason to keep fighting—whether it's faith, family, or a personal mission—you'll develop the resilience to push through even the toughest challenges.

4. **Find Your 'Why'**
   Wealth without purpose feels empty. Identify your 'why'—the deeper reason behind your goals. Whether it's creating a better future for your family, giving back to your community, or achieving personal growth, your 'why' will fuel your motivation.

5. **Strive for More—But Maintain Balance**
   Never become so focused on success that you sacrifice life's most precious moments. Family always comes first. When you prioritize balance, everything else will fall into place.

BIOGRAPHY

Guillermo Chávez-Angeles is an award-winning State Farm Agent, entrepreneur, real estate investor, and community leader. Originally from Guadalajara, Jalisco, Mexico, Guillermo began his professional journey in 2001 in the mortgage industry, helping individuals and families achieve homeownership.

During the recession, Guillermo entered the real estate market to help homebuyers navigate the market. He joined State Farm in 2014 and built a thriving enterprise with two locations and a team of twelve. Guillermo gives back to his real estate and Hispanic community as a dedicated leader in the National Association of Hispanic Real Estate Professionals (NAHREP), where he served as President of the DuPage chapter in 2021.

Guillermo Chávez-Angeles
Mexico

THE ATTORNEY

NANCY PIÑA-CAMPOS

"No one in my family had ever walked that path, and the idea felt like a distant star—bright and alluring, but far beyond my grasp."

When I was a little girl in third grade, a girl told us during recess, "Everybody put your hands in circle." We all obliged, excited to learn a new game. Then she said, "Whoever is not white, can't play." We all glanced at our hands that were touching side by side and I realized they were waiting for me to walk away. So, I did. It was an eye-opening and heart-breaking moment in my childhood. Up until that point, I had never felt different or less than others. But this moment, along with the time a boy in my fifth grade class didn't want me to sit at the same lunch table as him and yelled, "Get out of here you f_____ Mexican piece of____!" is when I realized, I was different.

Every bit of what makes me different is what makes me who I am today, and I can't explain it without mentioning my parents because their story, their culture, their struggle, and perseverance are woven into my being, and I am stronger because of it. My parents came to this country from Mexico with dreams of a better life, carrying the weight of their hopes and sacrifices on their shoulders. They worked tirelessly, often taking on multiple jobs, to provide for our family while maintaining their cultural identity.

From a young age, I witnessed the challenges they faced: the language barriers, the long hours, and the constant uncertainty that comes with being an immigrant. My father came alone to the United States, leaving behind my mother and brother. It was risky to cross the border to an unknown country without money, without speaking the language, and without a certain place to live, so they decided he would have to travel alone for the time being. The only thing he had was a plan: To succeed. My mother often shared stories of this time. How my brother would look at pictures of my dad and cry himself to sleep because he missed him so much. My father came to Chicago where he found work sweeping auto shop floors. He hoped to become a mechanic, but he had to work at it, literally, from the ground up.

Eventually my mother and brother were able to join my father in Chicago. They lived in rat-infested basements and had nothing more than each other. My father was working very long hours for very little pay. My mother also worked long hours in factories and then went to school at night to learn English. One day my father was fired from the auto repair shop. He was devastated and walked home thinking along the way about what he was going to do to provide for his family. He came across a building with a 'for sale' sign and dreamt of the possibilities if he would only be able to buy it. But how would that even be possible? He had no money, no job, no house of his own, but he did have resilience and determination—little did he know, that would suffice. A friend of his told him to look into the Small Business

Administration for a loan. He knew it was a long shot, but he prepared a business plan and applied. With hope in his heart, he waited for news of the loan and in the meantime, he came up with a name for his auto repair shop and designed his logo until the impossible finally happened—the loan was approved.

The year was 1980 when my parents purchased that first business and a couple years later, they were finally able to purchase their very first home in the Little Village neighborhood of Chicago. I was born in 1983 and that shop became my family's second home. Today, forty-four years later, my parents still have that same shop and also expanded to a second location in the 90s. The auto repair shop truly is a family business, and we have all worked there. My brothers were mechanics and then service advisors and managers. I was the secretary while in high school and then became the financial manager. Although my father never taught me how to rebuild a transmission, what I learned there became far more valuable throughout my life. I learned not only the day-to-day of how to run a business from the customer service aspect to the financials, but I learned that to be a business owner you have to have a strong support system and you have to take risks. What I learned in that shop was not from what I was being told—it's from what I saw. I saw pure determination and a fierce resilience from my parents that inspired me.

I was determined to excel academically, motivated not only by my ambitions, but also by my parents' sacrifices and decided to go to college—the first in my family to do so. I graduated with a degree in real estate investments and finance. I remember a classmate telling me he was going to go to law school, and I remember thinking how proud his parents must be, but not for a second did I think that it could be my reality one day. No one in my family had ever walked that path, and the idea felt like a distant star—bright and alluring, but far beyond my grasp.

I am not sure if it was the voice of that boy in the lunchroom calling me names or the little girl telling me I couldn't play because of my skin color. Maybe it was the Caucasian neighbors who would paste hate messages on my mom's car once we moved to a "nicer" neighborhood or perhaps the tv shows which never showed anyone who looked like us being anything other than a maid. Maybe it was everything—but without realizing it, all of these experiences built a wall in my mind telling me that I was not as good or as smart as the rest of my peers. I let five years pass until one day while working as a legal assistant, I told my brother, "I want to go to law school, but I'm old. By the time I graduate I will be 30!" His response was, "You will be 30 one day anyway, so you will either be 30 and still be the assistant to the attorney or you will be 30 and be THE attorney." He was so right. This was me, making excuses and putting up barriers as to why I couldn't do it, but it was time. It was MY time.

I went home that day and made my plan. I literally made a vision board. I did my research, and I wrote down the law school I was going to attend, the score I was going to receive on the LSAT, the year I would graduate, everything was on that board. While other young adults were visiting law schools with their parents, I was visiting them with my husband. It was my first year of marriage and more than once we were told that the divorce rate among law students was very high. We were told it was going to be a high stress environment and so much work that we would rarely see each other. We didn't know it at the time, but it would end up being very true. My husband is a carpenter and, back then, we were also dealing with the aftermath of the great recession. Needless to say, it was a very difficult time financially, but during a time when it really would have helped to have two incomes, my husband never questioned my decision to go to law school. Instead, he encouraged me and supported me financially and emotionally every step of the way.

Law school was every bit as stressful as they said it would be, but we survived. It was so intense and there were many students who dropped out the first and second year, but I had not come this far to quit now. During my last year of law school, I was pregnant with my first son. He was born on May 8th and I was actually in the hospital the day after giving birth finishing up one of my final papers. Ten days later was graduation and my newborn son was in the audience watching me receive my law school diploma (actually, he was sleeping, but the point is he was there).

The next two months were beyond exhausting, but this precious baby was my motivation to get through the long days in the library studying for the bar exam and the long nights with a newborn. The bar exam was in July, and it is two full days of testing. We need a new word for "stressful" to describe what it was like because that doesn't even begin to cover it. Two very long months later, in October, the results arrived by email. My baby was on the couch peacefully asleep, and my husband was at work. I saw the email had arrived and so I said a prayer before I dared to open it. I took a deep breath... "Congratulations..." That's it. That's all I was able to read. I fell to my knees and cried. Oh, how I cried. I cried tears of joy, of relief. Tears of gratitude and even tears of frustration. All the feelings I had felt during the past 10 years were released from my body in the form of tears. It had all been worth it.

I worked for a couple law firms at first because I wanted to get a feel for different areas of law to find what I really wanted to practice. I handled immigration cases, family law, criminal law and bankruptcy, but ultimately, I knew I wanted to return to my first passion, real estate, and so I opened my own law firm.

Now, as a real estate attorney, I dedicate my career to helping families make one of the biggest transactions of their lives—their homes. I understand the significance of this milestone, especially for immigrant families like mine. Every day, I strive to empower my clients with the knowledge and support they need to make informed decisions, and I do it in their language. It's more than just a transaction; it's about stability, security, and building a future.

Through my work, I aim to give a voice to those who might feel lost in the process, ensuring they are treated with respect and fairness. Each case is a reminder of my roots and the journey my family took to create a better life. I feel honored to guide others through their home-buying experiences, providing the support I wished had been available to my parents.

My journey as the daughter of immigrant Mexican parents has not only empowered me to become a lawyer but has also fueled my passion for serving my community. I strive to honor the legacy of resilience and hope that my parents instilled in me, ensuring that every family I work with feels supported and empowered in their journey to homeownership. It is my belief that the path to building generational wealth begins with homeownership. With education and the right guidance and leadership, we can take our families to the next level, and no one will be able to tell us again that we can't play because now… now we can all play.

TIPS FOR WEALTH & SUCCESS

Embarking on the entrepreneurial path is an exhilarating adventure filled with challenges and opportunities. Here are some tips to get you started:

1. **Find Your Love**

   Your passion will be your greatest motivator during tough times. When you genuinely care about your work, it shines through and resonates with others.

2. **Set Clear Goals**

   Define what success looks like for you. Break your long-term vision into actionable short-term goals. Celebrate small wins along the way. I created a vision board detailing every little thing I was going to achieve on my journey to becoming an attorney with my own law firm. If you write/draw it, then you just have to follow your map!

3. **Network Relentlessly**

   Surround yourself with like-minded individuals. Attend workshops, join entrepreneurial groups, and connect with mentors. Building a supportive network opens doors to new ideas and collaborations. Often times we are held back by all the voices that surround us from friends and family who don't understand our vision. Don't listen to people who are not where you want to be.

4. **Embrace Failure as a Teacher**

   Failure is not the end; it's a stepping stone to success. Each setback provides valuable lessons. Analyze what went wrong, adjust your approach, and keep moving forward with newfound wisdom.

Stay fierce, stay determined. Your dreams are valid, and you're capable of achieving them!

BIOGRAPHY

Nancy Piña-Campos is the founder and owner of Piña Law Firm, LLC. Her practice focuses on real estate transactions and estate planning.

Nancy graduated from DePaul University with a major in Real Estate Investments and Finance. She obtained her Juris Doctor from The John Marshall Law School, where she was president of the Real Estate Law Student Group, member of the Latino Law Student Association, member of Lambda Alpha International (Honorary Society for the Advancement of Land Economics), and member of the Trial Advocacy Honors Council. During this time, she also held an externship with the Neighborhood Housing Services.

Nancy's other work experience includes work as a Judicial Extern for The Honorable Lisa Marino of the Circuit Court of Cook County, Chancery Division, as a legal intern for Clarion Associates conducting research for the Argentinian Conservation Easement Project, and volunteer at the Domestic Violence Legal Clinic.

Nancy is a member of the Illinois State Bar Association, and she serves on the board of the National Association of Hispanic Real Estate Professionals (NAHREP) DuPage County Chapter.

She is licensed to practice law in the state of Illinois and is fluent in Spanish.

Nancy lives with her husband and three beautiful children.

Nancy Piña-Campos
Mexico

L'ECOLE, L'EGLISE, LA KAY

ALIX JUDE CHARLES, MD

"I had seen firsthand that even if a goal seemed lofty or difficult to achieve, it could be conquered with a solid plan and the willingness to put in the hard work."

My parents made me angry. More specifically, the way that they made my family, and by extension myself, so obviously different than everyone else in my neighborhood and elementary school is what made me angry. I didn't want to be different. I wanted to be normal, just like everyone else. I wanted to blend into the background and not stick out like a black spot of ink on a tapestry. In short, I wanted to be what I perceived to be "American."

I wasn't allowed to eat dinner or sleep over at my friend's houses. I had to come right home after school and immediately begin my homework instead of playing outside with the kids in the neighborhood. Even if I had something I wanted to do for myself on a Sunday, I knew I wouldn't get a break from the routine of church followed by family lunch and visiting with relatives. I was embarrassed by my parent's imperfect English and their ability to speak in a language different than my schoolmate's parents. Enjoying a baseball game at Wrigley Field with a hot dog and a coke in hand was a dream that never seemed possible given my reality; televised soccer matches at home and foods like fried pork or rice with beans are what I could expect instead.

My parents immigrated from Haiti in the late 1960's to escape the oppressive regime of a rising dictator named Jean Francois Duvalier. They had professions in healthcare that they hoped would offer them a chance at prosperity for themselves and the family they wanted to begin. In my younger days, I couldn't see outside myself to appreciate the courage and selflessness they showed by leaving their home to pursue the promise of a better future in a country so different from their own. I couldn't see it in my youth, but my immigrant birthright and the values that came along with it would be the steppingstones to my own American success story.

L'ecole, L'eglise, La kay. Translated from Haitian Creole these words mean School, Church, and Home, respectively. Any Haitian immigrant parent in the US will tell you these three places represent a world of options and a shelter from the dangers that can ensnare unsuspecting youth who wander into the wilderness of choices offered by Western civilization. These three places represent an anchor of consistency that permit the passage of cultural ideals like self-discipline, humility, respect for self and others, and love for oneself and one's community. To a young Haitian American growing up outside Chicago in the 80's, these three places were seen as confining, and as something that separated me from what I thought were the best things the US had to offer.

I've often said that being first-generation in this country affords a perspective and vantage point to immigrant children that natural-born American citizens sometimes find difficult to appreciate. My parents came from a country where political oppression and corruption within the ranks of government and business leadership meant that opportunities were restricted to the chosen few. Having this be their reality made it easier for them to see how special free speech, democratic elections, open pathways to entrepreneurship, and a free market for businesses really is. My parents helped me see how these things are open to all in America, and to realize how few barriers to success really existed in America. If you can't see this yet, then I pray the chapters in this book open your eyes to these possibilities.

My parents, whom you'll remember had careers in healthcare, took the entrepreneurship plunge and opened a Caribbean restaurant when I was in my early high school years. I worked in every position at that restaurant, from host to waiter to cook. I began learning business lessons like how shifting wholesale food prices could compress profit margins, and how consistency in product offerings can create loyal customers. My parents experienced the joys and the challenges of small business ownership, and I was learning right alongside them. For many reasons the restaurant didn't succeed and would eventually close. I focused on the negative points of this experience and decided that entrepreneurship was not for me and finding a "secure" job would be my goal. I decided to go to college at the University of Illinois Champaign-Urbana and pursue a career as a physical therapist.

The winter break during my sophomore year of college proved to be a turning point for me that I will remember forever. Two important things happened that would change my life trajectory and led to the mindset pivot that laid the foundation for the success I've achieved thus far. The first thing was that I found out that I had earned a "C" grade in one of my classes! For a kid who had always prided himself on getting honors level grades in elementary and high school, this was a terrible shock. I was "independent" and "grown up" living away for school and had only myself and my poor work ethic to blame.

The second thing was a conversation with my cousin in my car while parked in the lot outside of my parent's restaurant. We were talking about planning out our life's career and I was telling him how my plans to become a physical therapist were mostly on track. My cousin kind of smirked and let out a chuckle, prompting me to ask him what he thought was so funny. He proceeded to tell me that my motivations for choosing that career over medical school were wrong. He told me I was selling myself short and that I was just scared of the level of time commitment and academic study that becoming a physician would require. He said I was taking a shortcut that I was almost certain to succeed at instead of taking a longer and more prosperous path that was more difficult and carried a risk of failure. I was stunned. He had laid bare to me something I had been hiding from myself, something I kept lying to myself about.

The winter break revelations of 1993 taught me two things: 1) If you let your focus waver from your chosen path, it won't be long before life will choose for you a very different path. 2) Self-doubt and fear are generated from within your mind, but they can have a real effect on your reality when they change what you perceive your choices to be. This distorted reality can limit your ability to see and reach your highest potential.

These two revelations have a common thread that has become one of my most frequently given pieces of advice for achieving success: be willing to take the blame. The word blame has a negative connotation that makes people upset when you associate it with them. However, I view blame as another word for responsibility. I believe that any situation in which I find myself, I deserve part of the blame. It may be that I initiated a series of events that led to the situation, and thus bear a large part of the blame. It could be that I entered a situation at the tail end and had very little to contribute, so my share of the blame is smaller. When I find myself as part of an argument or a project that is not moving forward as was originally hoped, I stop to ask myself what role am I playing in the situation and what things about my involvement have been helpful or harmful.

I have learned that the only thing I can control is myself, especially my own thoughts, perceptions, and actions. I can influence other people by what I say or do to them, and sometimes I can influence other outcomes or objects by taking action against them physically. Even then I can't fully control what happens afterwards because those things are external to me. Drawing this distinction between the self that I can control and the non-self that I can only seek to influence, but cannot fully control, has been powerful. When I operate from a place of accepting my share of the blame I can be clear eyed about what I must do to contribute to an outcome, and regardless of what happens at the end I am positioned to learn and grow. This constant growth is the lifeblood of my success.

Following the winter break of my sophomore year I became determined to go to medical school. I put pen to paper and came up with a plan. This was one of the first times I used goal-setting to help myself work backwards from my desired endpoint and broke down a plan into the individual steps whose execution would most probably lead to my goal. I deliberately planned out the courses I would need to take the next three semesters, and in what order, to fulfill the requirements for schools to which I would apply. Once I started a course, I would formulate questions in advance of lectures that I could plan on asking during class. This was both for clarifying what I needed to learn, but also to help get me noticed by my professors. I would deliberately think of topics to ask about at my professor's post-lecture office hours, which showed them my initiative and made it easier for me to influence them to write me glowing letters of recommendation. You can imagine that another obvious benefit of this attention to my coursework were also excellent grades, something else I knew I would need to get into medical school.

I approached preparation for the Medical College Admissions Test (MCAT) with the same level of planning. I took a formal test preparation course to help me better focus on how questions would be formulated and understand the mechanics behind standardized tests. I spoke to others who had taken the test and done well, gleaning from them what study tricks they felt left them best prepared. I took mock tests that I photocopied from study guides at the library, honing my abilities to see and conquer the hidden structure behind standardized test questions. When the time came for me to take the exam, my preparation paid off and I achieved a very competitive test score.

Despite having followed my well-laid plan and successfully arranging all the elements needed to get admitted to medical school, I still had self-doubt. I doubted my ability to get into a top tier school and decided to only apply to schools in Illinois; good schools for certain, but none of them in the upper echelon. My cousin, once again, played a role in changing my mind. He told me to apply to a competitive school that he learned through his research was generous with financial aid and thus worth looking into. I was certain that I couldn't get admitted to Mayo Medical School but figured I would reach for the stars and see if this was in God's plan for me. That year, I was one of 4000 applicants who were whittled down to 400 interviewees from whom just 42 were chosen to become members of the incoming class. When I got a letter from them at my school dorm, my hands were trembling as I opened it. I could hardly contain my joy when I discovered that my planning and preparation had paid off with me being one of the 42 chosen! That year, with a 1% acceptance rate, Mayo Medical School had the lowest admissions rate out of all the medical schools in the country. Further, the acceptance letter detailed that I was being given a full tuition scholarship, meaning I would graduate without being crushed by debt.

None of this would have happened had I succumbed to the limitations I had imposed on myself. Instead, I had proven to myself that I could be so much more than I had dared to dream. I had seen firsthand that even if a goal seemed lofty or difficult to achieve, it could be conquered with a solid plan and the willingness to put in the hard work. There is a quote by the great American inventor, Thomas Edison, that embodies this, and I love to share it with others: "Opportunity is missed by most people because it is dressed in overalls and looks like work."

Medical school is as difficult as you have heard it could be, but with careful planning I persevered. I used the same tools that got me into Mayo Medical School to secure a training position to become a dermatologist, one of the most difficult specialties to be admitted into. Choosing this specialty was strategic; I chose it specifically because I saw the myriad opportunities it would afford me to serve my community, challenge myself to grow, and help me achieve material success and the security that comes with it. There are many more lessons that I learned along the way and sharing them all with you would require several more chapters! My hope is that what I have shared thus far resonates with you, the reader, and helps you to grow into your best self and maximize your potential.

TIP FOR WEALTH & SUCCESS

There is power in understanding that you are NOT your own thoughts, that who you are intrinsically is separate from the thoughts that you have. I want you to take a moment and sit somewhere comfortably and close your eyes. For the next ten minutes, pay attention to the thoughts that come and go in your mind. I want you to observe them the same way you might watch cars and trucks driving back and forth when you are standing on a street corner. You will slowly come to realize that you don't actively create many of these thoughts. They just bubble up and enter your mind without you asking them to be there. Then, for the last minute of this exercise, I want you to imagine yourself growing to gargantuan size, imbued with fantastic powers like the ability to fly or project fire from your hands. Whatever powers you deem fantastic and make your heart race. Then open your eyes and re-enter the world. This exercise can help you to realize that while you can't control every thought and emotion from entering your mind along your road to success, you can always control the thoughts you want to create for yourself. It is in this way that you can craft your own reality.

BIOGRAPHY

Alix J. Charles, MD, is a board-certified dermatologist with a passion for patient-centered, physician-directed medical care. Born in Chicago, Illinois, he is the son of immigrants from Haiti. He earned his bachelor's degree in Kinesiology from the University of Illinois in Urbana-Champaign. His career in healthcare began at the Mayo Clinic in Rochester, Minnesota, where he completed medical school and part of his residency before completing his training in dermatology at Rush University Medical Center in Chicago.

As the chairman of the Department of Dermatology at Duly Health and Care, he oversees 17 dermatologists and 17 physician assistants that are part of a 1000+ physician multi-specialty group that emphasizes efficient and high-quality patient care in Illinois, Indiana, Iowa, and Missouri. Dr. Charles' practice encompasses medical, surgical, and cosmetic dermatology, and he sees both pediatric and adult patients.

He is a past president of the Chicago Dermatological Society and the Illinois Dermatological Society and was awarded the Darrel J. Stremler Leadership Award for his role in growing and managing his department. He has a special interest in pigmentary disorders and minimally invasive cosmetic procedures utilizing injectable agents and energy-based devices.

Alix J. Charles, MD
Haitian-American

A "PENJAMENSE" REACHING FOR HER DREAMS

TERESA RIOS

"I only have two options: sit and cry for what I lost or wipe my tears, stand up, and move on."

November 20th, 1985, Penjamo, Guanajuato; it was the anniversary of the Mexican Revolution, our town was full of celebration. While my community rejoiced, I was filled with anxiety, patiently waiting at the bus station with my mother and brothers, Valentin and Pedro, ready to embark on a new journey, a journey to California.

It was a big step for us. We'd never traveled so far before. A mixture of excitement and sadness filled our hearts as we left our hometown, unsure when we'd return. We were eager to finally meet my father, Pedro Rios, who had emigrated to the United States when I was just eleven months old, returning for only two weeks before heading back to his job. His brief visits had left us longing for his presence.

After a short wait, we boarded the bus to Tijuana, the first step in our journey to a completely new life. After being on the bus for two or three days, we arrived in Tijuana to meet my uncle, Jesus, who would guide us to San Diego, California. At just eleven years old, I was thrust into a completely different world. Moving to my father's house in Los Angeles was a huge change, not only because of the new country but also because I was establishing a relationship with my father who I didn't have during the first 11 years of my life, which was a challenge for my siblings and me.

Just a few days after arriving in Los Angeles, it was time to face another challenge: school. I knew it would be difficult, not because I disliked school, but because I didn't know a word of English. The first day of school arrived and I was extremely nervous. I couldn't understand the teacher and felt extremely lost. Despite having English as a Second Language classes, I felt so helpless and unable to do classwork or even class assignments.

While in class I grew more and more anxious as I felt the stares of the other students around me. Feeling uncomfortable and singled out because of the language barrier, I failed to receive adequate support from my teacher and learned my first lesson on resilience and hard work. I started to see that the only way I would be able to pass the class was to put more effort into it and seek help from my classmates who in some way mirrored me, as they also had the same experience with the language.

After several months of difficulties and new experiences in Los Angeles I started to feel a wave of confidence and determination rooted in community. I realized that not only did I have difficulties understanding the language, but so did my siblings and my parents. Understanding our shared struggle gave me purpose. From that moment on I became determined to learn English and change the trajectory of our lives for the better.

As the years went on, I learned English, graduated from middle school and continued onto high school, watching my English improve. Although I was able to adapt to my environment and gain language skills necessary to get through school, I soon learned that it wouldn't be enough to get me to college.

While I was excited about higher education, I also had no idea how I would pay for it. My parents were extremely hard-working yet their minimum-wage jobs, paid in cash, would make it difficult to fulfill my dream of attending college. Thankfully, I was able to seek help at school with the college application process and started asking teachers and classmates for information on financial assistance for college expenses.

After learning how I could receive financial assistance for college, it was just a matter of waiting to receive a response from the college application I had sent. After several weeks I received acceptance to California State University Los Angeles—one of my best achievements. From that moment on, I felt like I was on the right track. I started college and attended for two years. To make ends meet, I took on a part-time job at a fast-food restaurant. It was there that I would meet my future husband, Roman. We dated, eventually got married and then welcomed our first daughter, Roxana.

After attending college for two years, I was forced to make a difficult decision. I had to drop out. While I was ambitious, I also understood that I wouldn't have the capacity to dedicate myself to college full-time as I had previously. After giving birth and being a stay-at-home mom, I realized I wasn't meeting my full potential, so I decided to re-enter the workforce. At that time, some of my brothers had gotten together to start a new business, a pallet business. I reached out to them and asked if they needed help in the office. They agreed, and I immediately started working with them, even though I had no prior knowledge of the industry.

After years of working alongside my brother, I decided to start my own pallet company in July of 2013. It was one of the riskiest decisions I had ever made, and eventually my husband quit his job to support me in this new venture. After making significant progress in the pallet industry and building a strong team with my employees and family, we were able to save enough money to buy a small piece of land to source the raw materials for our wooden pallets and even buy a new home.

Yet, this success wasn't without its challenges. In August 2019, we excitingly moved into our new home. Everything seemed to be going well until a sudden health crisis changed everything. After a routine medical exam, I had an accident that landed me in intensive care for two weeks. Being hospitalized was one of the most difficult experiences of my life. My family also struggled with my illness and the challenges of keeping the family business afloat, as I had always been the primary person in charge of our operations. Thankfully, my family learned to manage the business and kept it moving forward while I recovered.

Those days were incredibly stressful but after the years of work I had put into building a business I learned how valuable our health is. After a few weeks, I was able to return to work and keep moving forward. The company was growing, and we had to hire more people to keep up with demand for pallets. It's easy to lose control of a growing business, but I was determined to keep things on track and maintain steady growth.

My dreams were far from over, and there was so much to be accomplished. I knew of my goals and I was determined to achieve them. While we were experiencing major growth at the company life would soon throw us a curveball that would change the trajectory of our lives.

On February 26, 2021, I received a call from a neighbor who lived in the city of Compton where my company was located with the news that our business was on fire. It was around 4 a.m. when I got the call. The fire started in a nearby alley and quickly spread to a mattress company, then to another pallet company, and finally to ours. We rushed out of bed and headed straight to the office, trying to salvage what we could before the fire department arrived. Unfortunately, when we got there, everything was already destroyed. Our inventory of pallets and wood was gone, and we even lost a beloved pet. It was a devastating loss.

The fire impacted us in ways we could have never imagined. It represented a major loss of what we spent years building collectively as a family and once again my resilience and ability to rely on loved ones would be the most important path to healing. Our loved ones galvanized behind us and provided emotional support and we were tasked with rebuilding everything we once had. Unfortunately, just two months prior to the fire our fire insurance was terminated and thus we were left with no financial support or protection that would streamline our path to recovery.

Yet, we kept going. My family and I had no time to lose because our customers were waiting for their pallets, and we couldn't afford to lose them as clients. After losing our headquarters, we were without a formal office and had to use our car as a temporary office, taking calls for orders, parked in the front seat. I knew we had to find other ways to move forward and we were not short on being resourceful and innovative to meet demand. News spread and I received several calls from friends and colleagues in the pallet industry, helping in any way possible.

On one particular day, a frequent supplier who would regularly sell pallets to us shared an important observation on our resilience. The day of the fire, he came by and was shocked to see the destruction. He looked at me and said, "What happened? You're still working, even though everything's gone. You're so strong! If I were in your shoes, I'd be crying and devastated, but you're carrying on like nothing happened."

I told him, "I only have two options: sit and cry for what I lost or wipe my tears, stand up, and move on." He was truly impressed by my resilience.

Our community in Compton, California, supported me by giving me a hand during one of the toughest times in my life. Of course, the unconditional support of my family was invaluable. Having the support of my husband, daughters, and son meant that I couldn't give up. They've always seen me as a fighter, and this situation wouldn't stop me from moving forward.

After a few difficult months, we were able to rebuild Tere Pallets Corp. From working out of my car to relying on generators for power, we exhausted each and every method we could to continue running the business. Given the devastating loss, we set our sights on making a change in location that would decrease our susceptibility to fires and help us overcome the grief and sorrow of the tragic fire in 2021. After a few years, we finally did it. We bought a property and established a new headquarters for my multi-million-dollar business.

Despite the challenges we faced, one of the key themes and lessons of my life continues to be the power of community. The day we left Mexico, a day meant to celebrate revolution, marked the beginning of our own. We stepped into the unknown, my family and I, with only each other. What I discovered was the enduring strength of our bond and the unwavering support that allowed me to build not just a life, but a thriving multi-million dollar business that, like a phoenix, also rose from the ashes.

I want to dedicate this chapter to my family: Roman, Roxana, Jeanette, Michelle, and Albert. And, of course, my parents Pedro Rios and Maria Rios who risked everything to provide a better life for my brothers and I. And a special thanks to Guillermo and everyone who made this book a reality.

TIPS FOR WEALTH & SUCCESS

- Always bet on yourself and take risks that set you up for success.
- Don't be afraid of investing in yourself financially.
- Nourish a strong support system based on reciprocity.
- Resilience is key when starting your own business.
- Practice self-care regularly to build resilience over time.

BIOGRAPHY

Teresa Rios is a trailblazing entrepreneur from Guanajuato, Mexico, and the founder of Tere Pallets Corp. With over 30 years of experience in the pallet industry, she has carved out a leadership role in a traditionally male-dominated field. Her deep industry knowledge and unwavering commitment have propelled Tere Pallets Corp. into a globally recognized provider of high-quality pallet solutions.

Beyond her professional achievements, Teresa is a devoted mother and wife who values time with her family. She is also passionate about giving back to the community, actively supporting initiatives focused on education and environmental sustainability.

Teresa Rios
Mexico

UNSTOPPABLE: MY JOURNEY TO SUCCESS

LAURA RODRIGUEZ

"Obstacles are just a way of shaping you."

I sometimes stop and think about the future I could have had if my family hadn't moved to the United States. My future seemed predetermined—to marry young (as early as 15), raise children, and work the fields day in and day out. It was a cycle of poverty and silence. The options in our rural city of Tampico, Mexico, were limited and dreams were a luxury no one could afford.

I remember life was difficult as my mother cared for her ten children, including myself. My father worked in the US, sending back whatever little money he could. My mom used to sell freshly made cheese and I would help her by selling chili peppers on a passenger train. Life was about survival, not ambition. Education was scarce. While I was lucky to attend elementary school, I faced difficulties with the environment and authority figures. Even at a young age, I knew there had to be more to life than our reality.

Thankfully, when I was 11-years-old, I finally immigrated with my family to Chicago. My father and some of my older brothers and sisters had already been living in Chicago and it was my turn. They had left to pursue a life that would give us more than what we had in Mexico. Moving to the United States was one of God's greatest gifts for me, though it was filled with obstacles.

A NEW WORLD, A HARSH REALITY

When I stepped off the plane in Chicago, I carried nothing but a suitcase, my mother's prayers, and a heart full of hope. But hope alone wouldn't be enough to navigate the struggles ahead.

I started school in Prospect Heights, a suburb of Chicago, and I was the only Latina in my school. I didn't speak English and knew nothing about American customs. This made me open prey to the bullies of the school, who would speak to me in English knowing I couldn't understand them. The laughter of my classmates echoed in my ears, sharp and humiliating. I didn't understand their words, but I understood their intent. I was ridiculed and it ended in a lot of fights at school.

The bullying was relentless. Students mocked my accent, kicked my books, and humiliated me. I felt isolated and powerless, but pain became my motivation. I turned my pain into power. I refused to be defeated. Determined to learn English, I studied day and night. I stayed up practicing English, reading books aloud, mimicking words from the television. Within six months, I could stand in front of my class and speak fluently. Everything changed. I could finally defend myself—not just with words, but with confidence.

DREAMS BLOCKED, HOPE UNBROKEN

Luckily, my high school was a bit more diverse. Although school got easier, there still weren't a lot of options for me. I was expected to work while I was in school to help out with the family bills. I was also undocumented, since my travel visa had expired long ago. This made it difficult to go to college, since I couldn't get financial aid. Any classes I took would have to be paid in full. I also couldn't join the Army, since I wasn't a legal citizen. I continued to work though, trying to find ways to make my dreams come true.

When I was younger, I dreamed of being a journalist. I saw myself on TV being the news reporter and being a successful journalist. However, those dreams soon got lost, as more and more obstacles came between us. I was determined not to let these setbacks stop me from finding success in this country. I soon found that obstacles are just a way of shaping you.

After high school, I began working multiple jobs to help support the family. From factory worker to cashier to waitress, I tried it all. Nothing felt right, until one day I found a job as a teller at a bank. I worked full-time during the day and on weekends, and in the afternoons, I went to school. Even with two jobs, it was only enough to help my parents pay rent, pay for the train I took to college in Chicago, and return home at midnight. It was exhausting. Most nights, all I could afford were $0.99 fries from McDonald's to calm my hunger. Yet, hunger and exhaustion could not defeat my determination. I knew I was meant for more, and I wouldn't stop until I achieved it.

Working at the bank allowed me to see a whole new world of possibilities. While working there I was able to bring in a lot of new customers. They came in confused about mortgages, business loans, and credit scores, and I found myself eager to help them. My ability to translate not just Spanish, but the financial language, made me invaluable. I wasn't just cashing checks; I was unlocking doors. When I was promoted from teller to banker, I realized I had a gift for guiding others toward financial independence—something I desperately wanted for myself too. Working at the bank allowed me to see a whole new world of possibilities. I was hungry for financial independence and to branch out on my own.

TURNING STRUGGLES INTO STRENGTH

Life as an undocumented immigrant had a lot of obstacles. One time at the age of 17, while visiting family in Arizona, I was arrested in an immigration raid. Since I didn't have the right ID, they brought me to jail where I was able to make one phone call to one of my siblings to help me.

The metal cuffs were cold around my wrists as they loaded me onto the bus. I looked around at the hardened faces and hollow eyes, men murmured in hushed voices. I wasn't a criminal, but here I was, shackled among them; my fate uncertain. The bus screeched to a halt, and without a word, they pushed us out at the border near Nogales. The desert stretched out before me, vast and unfamiliar. My heart pounded as I prayed my family would come for me. I had never felt so alone. Thankfully, my brother-in-law, who was a US citizen, came and met me to take me home. I prayed my immigration status would change after this experience.

THE POWER OF PERSISTENCE

In 1992, my persistence paid off—I received my residency. Five years later, I became a U.S. citizen. That moment changed everything. I was no longer bound by limitations. I was free to pursue my dreams.

Over the years, my father saw how hard I worked. At first, he couldn't understand my hunger for independence. "A woman should be taken care of," he would say, shaking his head as I juggled multiple jobs and classes. But over the years, he watched me build something from nothing.

In 1996, at the age of 23, I bought my first home. He stood in the doorway, silent for a long time. Then, with teary eyes, he whispered, *"Estoy orgulloso de ti."* I knew then that he finally saw what I had been fighting for all along. He told me that he wished he had done more to support me earlier in my career, but who knows if I would be where I am today if I hadn't had certain challenges. I believe these things happen for a reason, and they work out the way God intended.

Then, in 1997, I took a leap of faith and started my own business. It was a risk, but I had nothing to lose and everything to gain. I was encouraged to get my real estate license by one of my bank customers. She told me I had a "thing" for helping others. That's when I began to find my true calling. I was able to help and guide families not only to achieve the American Dream of owning a home, but to guide them in a way that would make it possible to do things correctly. A dream that my parents could not achieved because they lacked guidance. My journey inspired others around me. One of my brothers and several friends followed in my footsteps, becoming realtors. Two other brothers left factory jobs to start their own successful home inspection businesses.

In 2000, my sister Elia and I decided to join forces to start our own business. We had both seen the difficulties our parents had faced in this country, especially when it came to taxes, financial advice, and legal services. Because of those difficulties, we decided to start a business that would help and guide our community. We opened our first accounting office, Alianza Hispana Inc. Now, we are celebrating our 25th year in business, and today, we have four thriving locations in Wheeling, Hanover Park, Elgin, and Round Lake. We built more than a business; we built a legacy of hope and opportunity.

TURNING PAIN INTO PURPOSE

Life tested me again and again. In 2016, my father passed away. Then, in 2021, my mother died. It was painful, but my parents had taught us resilience and responsibility. In 2022, tragedy struck once more—my brother died in a car accident. I was shattered. My world stopped. Family is everything to me. I am married with two children, and the fear of losing them overwhelmed me. But life is about loving what you do and cherishing your loved ones. I knew I had to keep going and moving forward.

In September 2022, my sister and I launched the first Mexican Wine Label in Chicago—a project dedicated to my father's memory. It was more than a business; it was a tribute to the sacrifices my parents made. We wanted to acknowledge our father's legacy that continues with our family.

Looking back, every hardship, every setback, every moment of doubt was part of a greater plan. The little girl who once felt lost in a foreign land became a woman who built a legacy for her family. I am proof that no dream is too big, no obstacle too great. I have a son, Sebastian, and a daughter, Laura Daniela, and as I watch them carve their paths, I hope they see that with faith, resilience, and relentless determination anything is possible.

Why do some people succeed while others don't? The answer lies in faith and perseverance. Dreams create paths. You must believe in change, and above all, you must have faith. Don't let anything or anyone hold you back. If you have the tools, keep going. If it's hard, find a way to change it.

My faith in God has helped lead me to where I needed to go throughout my journey. One Bible verse that reminds me of God's plan is: "Commit to the LORD whatever you do and He will establish your plans" (Prov. 16:3). I often made plans for myself, but they were not always what God had in mind for me. However, His plans got me to where I am now. He saw a path that I could not have imagined as a child living in Mexico. I'm grateful for all the obstacles I overcame to get me to where I am today.

To Sebastian and Laura, you will have regrets. That is part of growing, but there are more reasons to be grateful. Our past does not define us. We need to keep moving forward, or we may never find what we truly need. There is a plan for us, but we have to be open to receiving it. This doesn't mean it will be easy. You have to have faith and work hard towards what you hope to achieve. Just don't be surprised if your destination changes; it's all part of the journey.

TIPS FOR WEALTH & SUCCESS

One thing I have learned from my experience is that status does not define you. What I am today might seem small to some but monumental to others. What truly matters is how big or small you see yourself. We can push ourselves to do great things. When we let technicalities hold us back, we may miss out on opportunities that come before us. There is never a perfect time. I often stumbled past roadblocks, but I kept moving forward. Even though I couldn't go to college in the traditional way, I was able to find ways to pay for classes and better myself. All of this prepared me as an entrepreneur to solve problems I encountered along the way.

BIOGRAPHY

Laura A. Rodriguez is a proud and blessed Latina entrepreneur. Laura has been a business owner for over 27 years in the Chicagoland area.

Laura began her first business as an independent real estate agent in 1997, then Alianza Hispana Inc., with her sister in 2000. The business offers service support to the Hispanic community, guiding customers through tax preparation, notarizing legal documents, and home buying. This has helped those in the Hispanic community to overcome language barriers for services that help them to realize the American Dream. After 25 years, they have over six thousand customers and four locations, in Wheeling, Hanover Park, Elgin, and Round Lake.

In addition to owning her business, Laura has been a top producer in real estate for companies, such as Century21 and Re/Max. She is now planning on opening her own real estate office. She's motivated by helping others, by offering those who are willing the opportunity to be successful and work to build efficient teams using interpersonal and technical skills.

Currently, she volunteers and has been a member of many organizations, including the National Association of Hispanic Real Estate and Professionals. (NAHREP), Northwest Hispanic Chamber of Commerce, and Rotary Club of Wheeling.

Laura Rodriguez

Mexico

A LEAP OF FAITH
ELIA RODRIGUEZ

"I had to believe there was something more out there and find the strength to move forward."

I am a Mexican immigrant born in Tampico, Tamaulipas. I am the sixth of ten siblings who survived out of a total of fourteen. I am married to the love of my life, a mother of one daughter, and a grandmother to four grandchildren (one girl and three boys).

I lived and grew up in a small town in Tamaulipas, in a humble two-room wooden house that lacked many basic services, only having electricity. Located five kilometers from the main road, I would walk that distance daily to catch the bus that took me to school for middle and high school classes, a journey of about 45 minutes each way.

Due to economic hardships, opportunities were limited, and the effort to improve meant constant sacrifice. My parents, in their efforts to educate us and support our large family, would periodically migrate to the United States, where they worked for periods of one to two years. Thanks to the permanent residency obtained by one of my older siblings through his citizenship, they could come and go, always with the goal of providing for their children.

At the ages of 14 and 16, on two separate occasions, my parents had to leave me in charge of my younger siblings under the fragile protection of my maternal grandparents, thinking we were safe because our house was near theirs. All of this happened while my parents worked tirelessly in the United States, saving what they could to build a better house for us and continue paying for my education. I had been accepted into the university and could have become the first university graduate in the family. My parents' plan represented hope for a better future, though every separation was a tremendous sacrifice for everyone.

Those absences turned into challenging times, not only because of family separations but also due to the risks and dangers we faced because of our young ages. I bore the responsibility of caring for my siblings, who were 12, 10, and 8, while also attending school. However, despite the physical separations, love and family unity always prevailed, values that remain strong to this day.

Being on our own exposed us to a lot of dangers. It was during one of those absences that my youngest brother suffered an accident, which fortunately did not have fatal consequences. Given the seriousness of the situation and seeing the risk of danger their children were in, my parents made a momentous decision to return to Mexico, not to continue building our house, but to take us all to the United States in search of a better quality of life and to live together as a family without further separations.

That decision was, without a doubt, one of the bravest my parents ever made. It was a radical change that transformed our lives, opening doors to the many opportunities this great country offers and allowing us to finally live together as a united family in pursuit of a better future. However, for me, this wasn't the best news at the time. In fact, this new reality felt like a threat to everything I had achieved so far. I was already attending university and had fallen in love.

This was one of the biggest challenges of my life. I had to interrupt my studies in Public Accounting and Business Administration. My goal had always been to graduate and work to help my parents, who had sacrificed so much to pay for my education. Yet, due to my father's decision, I emigrated to the United States on July 23, 1984. This move not only meant leaving behind the love of my life but also made it impossible to finish my degree.

Thus, my life took an unexpected turn. Faced with an uncertain future, I felt a mix of uncertainty, sadness, and fear, but also hope and excitement for new opportunities and the warmth of family, though it came at the cost of the dreams I left behind and my romance at the time. I have always been a dreamer with aspirations. Although I didn't agree with my father's decision, I recognize that this country has given me the opportunity to achieve many accomplishments and fulfill my dreams. However, the path wasn't easy. Not knowing English and lacking guidance at the beginning were significant obstacles.

When we arrived in the United States and settled in an apartment, I realized that enrolling in a university or college was very difficult. Many requirements needed to be met, especially English proficiency, and education was costly. We didn't have the financial resources, and for my parents, it wasn't a priority for me to study. What was important was that my older siblings and I worked to contribute to household expenses while my younger siblings continued their studies.

I worked in various jobs. My first job was at a cable factory in Chicago, earning $3.35 an hour in 1984. A year later, I left to work as a housekeeper at the Embassy Suites Hotel in Schaumburg. It was hard work but paid better at $4.80 an hour.

Starting at the bottom, I was always determined to learn and gradually move up to better positions in every job I had. For example, I went from housekeeper to room supervisor, from factory assembler to quality control, and eventually to being an assistant of a Public Accountant, Don Ramon. That's when I realized that life was leading me to fulfill my passion, what I had studied and always loved doing: business accounting.

Shortly after moving to the United States, I met my husband and had one daughter. It wasn't long before I realized the marriage was not a partnership. I found myself unable to fulfill my own dreams of education and a career outside of my family. He literally stood in my way as I tried to leave for an exam, forcing me to stay at home and fail. After 14 years of a difficult marriage, I got divorced.

This divorce meant a change to another stage of my life and a new reality. Now I was alone with a daughter and had to strive for our financial future, but at the same time, a healthier one emotionally for both of us. In search of freedom and financial stability, I not only prepared myself to obtain a mortgage broker's license but also decided to start my own accounting business. Armed with the knowledge I had acquired while studying in Mexico and the experience gained as an assistant accountant—I took a leap of faith. The accountant I worked for encouraged me to pursue my own business.

In October 2000, alongside my sister and partner, Laura Rodriguez, and with a loan from a relative, we founded Alianza Hispana Inc., a company dedicated to tax preparation for small businesses and individuals. In addition to accounting services, we incorporated other essential services such as public notary, travel agency, auto insurance, and more, providing the guidance and support that immigrants, like our parents, needed when we first arrived in this great country.

At the beginning, I juggled running my own business, while also working for a mortgage broker and selling pots and pans on the side. The days were long, but I was making something for myself. I knew this is why we had moved to this country, because it allowed us the opportunity to build something of our own. Now that my daughter is grown, she is part of the family business and manages one of the branches. What I've created was never just for me, but is something that is able to be passed on to future generations.

Today, we have expanded and operate in four locations and serve a client base of over 6,000. This solid financial foundation allowed my sister and I, to officially launch ELLA Wines & Imports Corporation in 2022, a company dedicated to importing wines from Mexico with our own label. This new venture was created to honor the memory of our father, our hero.

Despite facing many challenges at the beginning, mainly the lack of sufficient financial resources to start my business, coupled with the discrimination I endured, very specifically during my previous marriage, where obstacles were imposed on me as a woman that hindered my educational, professional, and entrepreneurial progress—I persevered. There have always been obstacles, but it has been up to me to find a way around them. Even in my darkest days before my divorce, I had to believe there was something more out there and find the strength to move forward.

My resilience and determination to take control of my life and build my own destiny have allowed me to overcome the fears I had when I arrived in this country, which I now consider my home. This marked a turning point, teaching me that regaining my self-esteem, staying focused on my dreams, and facing every challenge with courage are fundamental steps to moving forward. With faith in God and a heart full of gratitude for the opportunities I've been blessed with, I've learned to celebrate every achievement—big or small—as a testament to the truth that anything is possible when it's planted in the minds and hearts of those who face similar challenges.

Today, being a proud citizen of the United States, I understand that the hardest barriers are not external but the ones we create ourselves from our fears, insecurities, and doubts. Freeing ourselves from those internal limitations is what truly allows us to reach our fullest potential.

TIPS FOR WEALTH & SUCCESS

My biggest tip for wealth and success is to put love into whatever you do. I was never focused on being successful. I was focused on love—love for my family, love for my community. I wanted to provide a better life for my daughter, which she can pass down to my grandchildren. That is my greatest success, knowing that what I did will live on through them.

Always remember its possible to do whatever you want to do. The important thing is to keep finding a way to move forward. When I was working three jobs, I was just focusing on moving forward. I wasn't thinking about how someday I could be a successful entrepreneur with two businesses. Focusing on what I could do in the moment for those I loved has brought me to where I am now.

BIOGRAPHY

Elia Rodriguez is an entrepreneur and the co-founder of Alianza Hispana Inc., an accounting firm with four locations: Wheeling (established in 2000), Hanover Park (2003), Elgin, and Round Lake Heights (2018).

In November 2021, she ventured into the wine industry by co-founding ELLA Wines & Imports Corporation with her sister and officially launched in September 2022. This wine label features artisanal wines exclusively sourced from the vineyards of Baja California, Mexico. This groundbreaking achievement led The Daily Herald to recognize them as the "First Latina Women to Own a Wine Label in Chicago in the year of 2022."

Elia is a Licensed Loan Originator at Emerald Mortgage Corp. She serves on the Advisor Committee for the Northwest Hispanic Chamber of Commerce.

She previously held the position of Government Affairs Director for the National Association of Hispanic Real Estate Professionals (NAHREP) DuPage County Chapter and completed a two-year term as President of the Northwest Hispanic Chamber of Commerce.

Elia Rodriguez
Mexico

A LEGACY OF GRIT, GRACE, AND GIVING BACK

Sisters Elia and Laura Rodriguez were not born into wealth or handed a clear roadmap for success. What they did inherit was something far more powerful: the courage, determination, and unwavering values instilled by their immigrant parents. In 2000, fueled by the challenges their family faced when they first arrived in the United States, Elia and Laura co-founded Alianza Hispana Inc., a tax preparation and general services firm dedicated to helping their community navigate the very systems that once felt inaccessible to their own family.

At the time, both sisters were unmarried, and Elia was raising her daughter as a single mom. Securing funding wasn't easy, and traditional lenders weren't willing to take a chance on them. Yet, they leaned on faith and family—securing a loan from their eldest sister's brother-in-law to launch their dream. It wasn't just a business loan—it was a vote of confidence, a sign that even when the odds were stacked against them, they weren't alone.

They brought with them knowledge, education, and lived experience, but more importantly, they brought heart. Alianza Hispana was built not just to offer services—it was created to offer hope. Over time, that hope multiplied. What started as a small venture has now grown into four locations, two of which the buildings are owned by the sisters themselves. Through Alianza, they gained something that generations before them had only dreamed of: financial freedom—and with it, the ability to dream even bigger.

In 2016, when their beloved father passed away, the sisters were moved to honor the man who had taught them the value of hard work, love, and sacrifice. They reflected deeply on how best to celebrate his legacy. What emerged was more than just a business—it was a heartfelt tribute. In 2022, Elia and Laura launched ELLA Wines & Imports Corporation, becoming the first Latinas to own a wine label in Chicago.

Thanks to the steady growth of their first business, Alianza Hispana, the sisters were eventually able to purchase a warehouse to support their wine distribution. It's something they're deeply proud of—especially because they've been able to pay the building and wine off completely, without relying on loans.

Their wines, imported from some of Mexico's most celebrated vineyards, are a symbol of celebration, of love, of heritage—and of a promise kept to their father.

Today, ELLA Wines & Imports Corporation and Alianza Hispana Inc. stand as twin beacons of resilience, vision, and sisterhood. They are not just businesses—they are bold declarations that immigrant women can build empires, that love for family can shape futures, and that giving back to your community is one of the most powerful legacies of all.

TURNING SETBACKS INTO STEPPING STONES

PABLO SARMIENTO

"Every setback is an opportunity to learn, and every obstacle is a chance to grow."

I don't remember much of my time growing up in Ecuador, and even the pieces that come to mind aren't all that vivid. From what I do remember, there were long, winding walks to and from school, sometimes in the heat and sometimes through the rain. It was a quiet life, one shaped by routine. Mornings would start early, my sister and I would gather our things, and we would make our way through the then-familiar streets of our neighborhood. The sights and sounds of Ecuador became white noise to me—the laughter of kids playing outside, the smells of street food vendors selling everything from empanadas to fried plantains, and the vibrant colors of the markets bustling with life. Even though my parents weren't physically with me, I felt connected to my roots.

But that connection was a double-edged sword. Early on, my parents made the tough decision to leave my older sister and me behind in Ecuador while they took my baby brother and ventured to this distant place called America. I didn't fully understand what was happening at the time—all I knew was that my parents were gone, and we were still here. They went in search of something better, something bigger. This place they spoke of with such hope and determination, America, was meant to be the land of opportunity, where dreams became reality.

They left with the goal of making it home. But, for me, home was Ecuador. Home was the streets I walked, the language I spoke, and the people I grew up with.

The absence of my parents was hard. Growing up in a whole country away from them meant a significant void in my life. I didn't have the comfort of family dinners where we could all sit around the table and share stories about our day. There were no weekend outings, no family vacations, no parents to tuck me in at night when I felt scared or lonely. It was just my sister and me. I had to learn quickly how to cope with that absence. I had to rely on myself, on my daily routine of going to school and coming back home. It wasn't the life I imagined, but it was the life I knew.

That life in Ecuador lasted until I was in second grade. And then, out of nowhere, everything changed. Suddenly, I was no longer in the only place I had ever known as home. I was uprooted, taken from Ecuador, and thrust into a brand-new world that was nothing like what I had experienced before. I didn't just move to a new house or a new neighborhood—I moved to a whole new country with a completely different culture, language, and way of life. America was no longer this abstract idea that my parents had spoken of—it was my reality. But it wasn't just America; it was Pilsen, a vibrant yet tough neighborhood on the south side of Chicago.

Coming to America was a culture shock, to say the very least. My native language, Spanish, no longer fit the new world I had to get accustomed to. The friendly "*hola*" I had used every day in Ecuador was replaced by "hello." "Casa" became "home," and Ecuador became a distant memory as I navigated this strange, fast-paced life in America. And, as if that wasn't hard enough, I was dropped into second grade—only this time, in an American school where I didn't know the language, the culture, or anyone around me.

Second grade was incredibly difficult. In fact, it was so hard that I had to repeat the year. It wasn't just the academics that were tough—it was the entire experience of trying to fit in when everything around me felt foreign. The classroom was filled with kids who spoke English fluently, and here I was, struggling to understand even the most basic instructions. I felt like an outsider. I felt lost. But, looking back, that experience made me stronger. It made me adaptable.

I guess you could say I became an expert in second grade, having gone through it twice. By the time I reached third and fourth grade, I had started to find my footing. I made friends, settled into the neighborhood, and began to learn the ropes of my new environment.

But even though I had started to adapt, things weren't easy. Growing up on the south side of Chicago came with its own set of challenges. While I was still a kid, trying to navigate the usual trials of childhood—bullying, peer pressure, and fitting in—there was an additional layer of difficulty. I was the only Ecuadorian kid in a school filled with predominantly Mexican students.

That set me apart, made me different, and in the eyes of some kids, made me a target. Bullying became a constant, and with it came the pressure to fit in, to belong.

Moving around a lot within the neighborhood didn't help either. We were constantly on the move, and with each move, I found myself crossing the invisible but very real boundaries between rival gang territories. Gang violence was pretty present in Chicago culture at the time, and even though I was just a kid, I was already being stopped in school hallways and asked which gang I represented. The pressure was real. I had to make choices I didn't want to make, but there was always the feeling that I had to pick a side—even though I never wanted to.

By the time I entered high school, I had already been exposed to more than most kids my age.

My parents did their best, but they were also trying to navigate their new lives in America. My mom worked long hours in a factory, and my dad had a janitorial job downtown. They were focused on making a life for us, but that meant I didn't always have the guidance or support I needed during my more difficult moments. I started bringing home academic letters — detention notices, bad grades, and calls from teachers about my behavior. My parents didn't know how to handle it, and I don't blame them. They were doing their best with the tools they had. They were new to this life too.

Things came to a head during my freshman year of high school. One day, a sophomore student came up to me and started a fight. I don't remember all the details of what led up to it, but I do remember the aftermath—another call home. This time, my mom decided that something had to change. She started taking me to our local church, where she learned about a program for troubled youth in Omaha, Nebraska. And just like that, my life was set to change again. I didn't know what to expect, but I was willing to give it a shot.

Around the same time I started the youth program in Nebraska, my dad received devastating news—he had been diagnosed with cancer after collapsing at work. The diagnosis was a shock, but my dad kept going, kept working, and we all hoped for the best. I focused on the program, determined to make it work so that I could come home and be better. But a few months into the program, I got the call I had been dreading — my dad had passed away.

I was granted leave to attend his funeral, and I returned to the program after that. But things had changed. I had changed. The grief weighed heavily on me, but I knew I had to keep going. I wanted to finish the program, to make my dad proud, but when I turned 17, I was given the option to leave early. If I stayed, I was guaranteed a full-ride scholarship to the University of Nebraska. Or I could choose to leave. So, I did. I dropped out of the program, not fully understanding what that decision would mean for my future. I went back home, back to Chicago, and found myself falling deeper into the mindset I had before.

I was at a dead end. My life felt like it was spiraling out of control, and I couldn't see a way out. I remember being so caught up in my head when one voice happened to break through to me.

His name was Phelps. He was the one who made me realize that it wasn't too late, that I could still turn things around. I remember telling him how hopeless I felt, how I thought my life was over, and he simply said, "It's already alright." Those words stuck with me. They made me realize that I didn't have to be defined by my past mistakes. I could still take control of my life and change its course. I still think about Phelps and how that conversation changed my perspective.

From that moment on, I started making different choices. I stopped hanging around the wrong crowds. I stopped feeling sorry for myself and playing the victim. I wanted more out of life, and I was willing to work for it. Through my journey, I've learned that mindset is key. It is the foundation upon which success or failure rests. You cannot wait for life to change on its own—you must actively work to shape your perspective, your habits, and your responses to the challenges you face.

I was determined to rise above the circumstances of my past and the environment I grew up in. I realized that to do that, I had to invest in myself in every way possible. I started focusing on personal growth—reading books, attending workshops, and seeking out mentors who could guide me along the way. I developed the discipline to set goals and follow through on them. This was when I truly began to understand the importance of mental, emotional, and spiritual well-being.

Entrepreneurship, like life, is a mental game. You need to be resilient, adaptable, and constantly learning. Starting my own business was one of the hardest things I've ever done, but it also taught me the most about myself. It showed me that I am capable of overcoming obstacles, not just because I'm determined, but because I've trained my mind to see those obstacles as opportunities for growth.

As my life changed from feeling like a loser and feeling hopeless, I slowly started to see positive changes happening in my life. I now had positioned myself with new friends and acquaintances. During this time of change I had the privilege of meeting a beautiful, sweet, kind and smart young lady named Gina Diaz who today is my wife. Meeting Gina at this point in my life was life changing not only because I had someone in my corner who inspired me to be the best version of myself but because I felt true love for the first time ever.

Together we embarked into the world of entrepreneurship and learned to navigate the world of business and saw how important it is to have a solid like-minded team. Today thanks to the lessons, challenges, mistakes and opportunities I can truly say I found happiness and success.

Looking back and seeing all that I have been able to accomplish has truly set me on a path I wish I had had as a kid. I've accomplished getting my managing broker's license, investing in real estate not only for myself but for my children, and leading Hispanic Investor Network among others. My life has come full circle, as now I am able to be the leader and someone others are looking up to, just like I needed when I was going through the hard times.

The journey from Ecuador to Chicago, and from lost youth to entrepreneur, was not linear. It was filled with ups and downs, moments of self-doubt, and times when I questioned everything.

But through it all, I learned that the key to success lies in how you handle the challenges life throws at you. Every setback is an opportunity to learn, and every obstacle is a chance to grow.

The most important lesson I've learned is that success is not just about financial gain or professional milestones—it's about personal growth and fulfillment. It's about building something that aligns with your values and brings value to others. It's about creating a life where you can be proud of not only what you've accomplished but who you've become in the process.

Ultimately, my story is not just about entrepreneurship or overcoming adversity; it's about the power of the human spirit to adapt, to grow, and to thrive. It's about realizing that your past does not define you, and your future is shaped by the choices you make today. It's about understanding that success is not an endpoint but a continuous journey of learning, growing, and becoming the best version of yourself.

TIPS FOR WEALTH & SUCCESS

Becoming a successful entrepreneur is difficult, and I won't sugarcoat it. Anything worth achieving requires hard work, sacrifice, and persistence. There will be challenges, and many of them may be ones you create for yourself, like I did. Overcoming those self-imposed obstacles was the first step in my journey. To move forward, I had to stop seeing myself as a victim. I had to shift my mindset and see life as something working for me, not against me. This change in perspective wasn't easy, and some days it still isn't.

However, I've learned that your mindset is everything. You have to actively work on controlling your thoughts and emotions because they shape how you see the world and what you can achieve. Success doesn't come overnight, and it certainly doesn't come without struggle. The most important investment you can make is in yourself—mentally, emotionally, and even spiritually. A positive mental state doesn't just make life easier to handle; it creates the foundation for everything you want to accomplish. Remember, personality determines your reality. When you invest in cultivating a positive outlook, you'll find that your external world begins to change in ways you couldn't have imagined.

BIOGRAPHY

Pablo Sarmiento, born in Ecuador and raised in Chicago, is a proud husband and father of three with a passion for real estate, health, and fitness. He overcame significant challenges early in life, and these experiences shaped his resilience and determination.

With over 15 years in the real estate industry, Pablo is the Managing Broker of Diaz Case Realty. His success as a full-time real estate agent led him to become a full-time real estate investor, and he is now the founder and CEO of Investor GC. This general contracting company helps other investors with their contracting needs.

Pablo's years of expertise have allowed him to grow a robust real estate portfolio, but his impact extends beyond his business. He is deeply committed to giving back to his community, particularly by mentoring young men who lack father figures. Through his guidance, he helps them find direction and success in life. Pablo's energy, enthusiasm, and leadership make him a standout in his industry, while his dedication to helping others makes him a valued community member. His ability to lift others while continuing to grow his career defines the kind of leader and role model he strives to be.

Pablo Sarmiento
Ecuador

MADE IN KOREA: BUILT IN THE USA

TAMMY KIM HAJJAR MILLER

"Success isn't just about what you earn, it's about what you give."

THE WEIGHT OF FIVE BLANKETS

The night before we left Busan, South Korea, my mother packed five Korean blankets, thick with the weight of home. They smelled like our ancestors' prayers, like the rain-soaked air of the marketplace, like the whispered dreams my mother never spoke aloud. Each fold was careful, deliberate, as if she was tucking away something sacred—memories that we could only carry in our hearts, a familiar land we wouldn't be able to return to.

We left behind a life people would have envied—successful businesses, familiar streets, neighbors who had known us since I was born. A home that overlooked the city, where the morning light streamed through our windows like liquid gold. But envy is a fragile thing, easily shattered by the sharp edges of reality.

My mother knew that in Korea, a half-American daughter would always face a door that refused to fully open. The glances, the whispers, the unspoken judgment that hung in the air like thick smoke—these were the invisible walls built around us, pressing tighter as timed passed. So, she did what she had to, she adapted. She gathered what she could carry, not just the blankets, but her unshakable will, and we stepped onto that plane bound for America.

She didn't know if we were leaving for a *better* life. Only that we were leaving for a life. In her mind, survival was never about wanting more, but about taking what we had and molding it into a legacy our ancestors would be proud of.

THE CURRENCY OF GRIT

Chicago in the winter of 1976 was an unrelenting force, the wind sliced through our fashionable winter coats as if to remind us we were outsiders. My mother had dressed for Korea's mild winters, not the biting cold and windchill of the Midwest. But weather was the least of our concerns, our first priority was survival.

My mother took a server position at Kinzie Steak House, where the weight of a tray on her arm became the weight of our future. She worked long shifts, carrying plates steaming with food she would never taste, smiling at customers whose language she didn't fully understand. Her hands, once adorned with rings from her life in Korea, were now calloused from double shifts. Every night, after her shift, she would take the 36 Broadway bus home, then sit at the kitchen table to count her tips, separating them into neat stacks.

"Half for today, half for tomorrow," she murmured, almost like a prayer. I remember asking her about it one day. She looked at me, her eyes steady, "It's not how much you make, it's about how much you keep. Money is like time, Tammy, you never see how much you've wasted until you have none left."

By 1979, her discipline turned into bricks and mortar. She purchased her first building in America, a three-story building with a restaurant in the basement, a retail space on the first floor, and our home on the second floor. There was no car, no luxury, just long walks searching for the next opportunity and a silent prayer that continued focus and sacrifice would bloom into something greater.

At five years old, I learned numbers by watching my mother count change at the Maxwell Street Flea Market. My first classroom was a makeshift booth selling silkscreen T-shirts. My first drama series was me watching criminals distract my mom on one side of her display while their partner stole from the other side. I wasn't learning to spell "entrepreneur," but I was living its meaning—watching, absorbing, knowing that survival was an equation of risk and adaptation.

My mother never called herself a businesswoman, but now I know she was an all-around Boss Babe—a strategist, an economist, a negotiator—long before I understood what any of those words meant.

THE LESSONS IN AN AMERICAN GROCERY STORE

By 1984, our business had evolved into *Happy Food Spot,* a corner grocery store nestled in the Lincoln Square neighborhood. The name wasn't just optimism; it was strategy. "Americans like to be 'happy,'" my mother reasoned, as if a name alone could draw prosperity.

That store became my second home. I did my homework between the aisles of milk and bread, and memorized customer preferences before I learned algebra. Our world was measured in inventory counts and the buttons on the cash register.

"You must *always* think of people—how they act," my mother reminded me as she stocked the shelves. "They may change their mind a lot, but one thing is always the same—they eat. And when the food is gone, they will need to buy more."

When big-box stores like Jewel-Osco and Dominick's threatened our existence, my mother accepted the challenge. "They don't have what we have," she said with quiet confidence. "We *know* people. We see them. We *listen*." She pivoted—carrying specialty foods from Germany, Switzerland, and France, even adding delivery services before it was common practice. Of course, I was the delivery girl. She understood something that no business textbook could teach: money follows service.

But life isn't just business. It throws unexpected lessons at you, ones that don't fit neatly into a ledger. In 1990, when I was sixteen, I found out I was pregnant.

REDEFINING THE AMERICAN DREAM

I had never seen my mother so lost as when she found out I was pregnant. Not when she left her home, not when she worked sixteen-hour shifts, not even when business was slow. "You stupid girl. How could you throw it all away?" she barked, her voice sharp, but her eyes wet with unshed tears.

Her question wasn't cruelty. It was grief. It was fear. The news shattered her dreams. To me, it was a challenge. And I accepted it.

I moved out, took a job at Baker's Square, and juggled motherhood with school. People looked at me and saw a girl with a ruined future. What they didn't see was the woman I was becoming—the one who would then graduate from Saint Ignatius College Prep on schedule, my daughter, Cheyenne, in the audience. I refused to let circumstances define me.

I had inherited my mother's grit. And now, it was my turn to build something greater.

THE POWER OF THE PIVOT

My first semester at Loyola University was a disaster. I struggled. I failed. And I wanted to disappear. But quitting wasn't an option. So, I pushed forward. I enrolled in Harold Washington Community College, worked full-time as a legal secretary, and built my education in the small batches of time between work and motherhood.

By 1997, I had my degree from DePaul University with a major in accounting, a minor in finance. It was more than a diploma; it was proof that the baby was the blessing. That I had *what it took.* That my story would be mine to write.

After years of working, pivoting, and learning, I found my true professional calling in 2005, the mortgage industry. For the first time, all those years stocking shelves, balancing books, and reading people's needs made sense. I wasn't just selling home loans; I was helping others find their piece of the American Dream.

But personal dreams often take unexpected turns. Two weeks before my 40th birthday, my marriage ended.

THE SECOND CHAPTER

Starting over at 40 wasn't in the plan. But then again, neither was becoming a teenage mom.

God, He's funny like that.

At 43, I married Bernie.

A man who didn't just understand my story, he wanted to build the next chapter with me. Together, we blended our families, our ambitions, our drive. Cheyenne,

Isabel, Henry, Nicholas, Harrison—our children—became the heart of our home, a testament that family isn't only through blood, but about love that shows up.

And together, we built something greater. We built not just careers, but a *six-figure marriage*—one rooted in faith, execution, and a belief that the right partnership is the foundation for a *vibrant and thriving life.*

By 50, I had surpassed what I once thought was impossible - reaching a seven-figure income, giving away over $100,000 to charity - and proving that success isn't just about what you earn. It's about what you give.

A LEGACY IN MOTION

My mother retired in 2005 in the only way she knew how, with class and style. She bought a million-dollar condo on Michigan Avenue, and a luxury car that fit the years of sacrifice behind it.

Her life continues to be an example of adventure, contribution and heart. She has traveled to over 60 countries, and a few years back, donated her home in Korea (valued at $2 million) to the Catholic Church, ensuring single mothers and orphaned children had a place to grow.

Her empire wasn't built with privilege. It was built with five Korean blankets, $300, and an unbreakable will.

Now, I see that same fire in my children. They carry the legacy of an immigrant's dream, woven into their DNA, whispering that nothing is impossible.

People often ask me how I did it, how I navigated teenage motherhood, built a multi-million-dollar business, forged a second chance at love. The answer is simple: I never stopped moving forward.

Life isn't meant to be lived in hesitation. It is meant to be *lived fully*—with grit, with purpose, with the unwavering belief that the best chapters are always ahead.

And now, I ask you, what dream is whispering inside you?

Your future is calling. Answer, don't let it keep ringing.

Thank you for allowing me to share the journey God has blessed me with thus far – and I look forward to hearing yours one day too!

Until our paths cross again, I leave you with my life motto: "Have Fun, Make Money & Make a Difference."

TIPS FOR WEALTH & SUCCESS

Top 10 Tips for a Successful Life:

1. Love harder
2. Read every day
3. Pray with your family
4. Dream bigger
5. Do the work
6. Get professionally coached
7. Be generous and kind
8. Keep a tidy home
9. Travel the world
10. No health, no wealth

BIOGRAPHY

Tammy Kim Hajjar Miller is a powerhouse entrepreneur, mortgage expert, business coach, and triathlete who has built her success on the foundation of resilience, vision, and hard work—values she learned firsthand as an immigrant raised by a determined single mother. In 1976, Tammy and her mother emigrated from South Korea with little more than a dream and an unshakable work ethic. Watching her mother build a real estate portfolio from the ground up, Tammy developed a deep belief in the power of homeownership to create generational wealth.

A graduate of DePaul University's Business School with a degree in Accounting and Finance, Tammy found her calling in mortgage lending—a perfect blend of numbers and people. Since 2005, she has helped over 2,000 families secure home loans nationwide and now coaches modern-day loan officers across the United States on how to build sustainable and thriving mortgage businesses.

In 2017, Tammy and her husband restarted their real estate and investment portfolios from scratch. Through BIG dreams, relentless work, and unwavering faith, they rebuilt their success and now use their journey to inspire others. Now together, they run a marriage consulting and coaching company that helps career-driven professionals create a six-figure marriage, so they can live a seven-figure vibrant life—proving that wealth and happiness go hand-in-hand when built with intention.

A firm believer that success is not just about business, but about adventure and endurance in all areas of life, Tammy has also completed three triathlons, embodying the discipline and perseverance she teaches.

Tammy Kim Hajjar Miller
South Korea

RESILIENCE

ANTONIO JOSE SARMIENTO

"I know it sounds like a cliche but it's so true, without good health nothing matters."

I would like for you to try and understand a little bit of who I am to better understand what obstacles I personally overcame to get to where I am and where I plan to go.

My story begins in Chicago, IL, where I was born. I am a God-fearing family man. I am first generation, as my family immigrated to the U.S. from Barranquia, Colombia, over 50 years ago.

Growing up in my household was very similar to other immigrant families with their American-born child trying to help navigate them through the American ways. It brings a smile to my face when I think about it because I see it as a privilege to be born in this great country with immigrant parents. You get the best of both worlds and, if you're lucky, you learn more than one language!

My father, Roberto Sarmiento, came here with a bachelor's degree in science and experience as a microbiologist in Colombia. He later on finished his master's degree and pursued a PhD, but that never came to fruition. He worked in many Chicago hospitals as a microbiologist. He was a very hard worker. At times he balanced two full-time positions and the family to try and bring extra money in the household to help with expenses.

My mother, Humbelina, and my sister, Lissette, came a year after my father had a stable position and a place for them to live. My mother came with a high school education and was mainly a factory worker, but nonetheless she worked 40-50 hours a week for most of her life before she retired—in addition to cooking and cleaning daily and raising my sister and me. She is an amazing woman and was the backbone of our family.

I was born a couple years after my family relocated to the U.S. My mom told me recently that when she was pregnant with me when they were visiting Los Angeles, California, and were thinking of staying there. Man, my life would have been so different. I am glad they decided not to stay! I love Chicago.

My family had so many struggles as we all do. We dealt with a lot of racism as my parents chose to live on the northside of Chicago that at the time was mainly of one type of demographic. They refused to live anywhere else. They worked their butts off to make sure we could afford a stable life there and have a good education.

Through the years I noticed my father talking about an export/import business idea he had. He wanted to stop working 50-80 a week for someone else and start his own business.

He had this fire inside burning to own something of his own. He started several companies in his lifetime, but none of them ever became successful. He always told me, "Having a job and a consistent paycheck is good, but it would be better if you could control your own future and income." I never had the same sentiment. When I was of age to work, all I wanted was a stable job. Make some money to hang out with my friends, take out the girls, you know? The fun stuff. Who would have thought that I would be where I am today owning several businesses? I know he would have been proud.

Now that being said, having my own businesses didn't happen overnight and came with its own obstacles. After I graduated from elementary school, I was diagnosed with Type 1 diabetes. That was a shock as I had to try and change my eating habits and be more active, not to mention taking five-to-six insulin shots a day. Unfortunately, I never listened to my doctors and family members about taking better care of myself and what would happen if I didn't.

My parents did their best to guide me, but they worked so much so we could have more that I did and ate whatever I wanted. They didn't really know. Well, it caught up with me after high school. Through my twenties and thirties, I have had laser treatments for bleeding in the back of my eye, some nonreversible nerve damage to my feet, kidney damage that grew to kidney failure, and that's just to name a few. I got a list!

In my mid-twenties I started to work for a small, but well known and growing automotive company, where I learned a lot more about business, systems, structure, communication, marketing, etc. During my time there I was diagnosed with kidney disease. I was horrified! Not to mention the effect it had on my family. After several years at this company and learning how to deal with this serious disease, on top of my diabetes, I was at a crossroad at work. I made some regrettable decisions with my team at work that got me into some hot water and they were also making some serious changes to my position as Business Development Manager due to them being acquired. I was given the option of being let go or taking a lesser position as a salesperson, which I did not want to do. Remember what I said earlier, stable job equals stable income.

Anyhow, my wife at the time had been begging me to leave that business for several years before I came to a crossroad as I saw my own health deteriorating due to the stress, hours, and my poor eating habits I was accustomed to. She kept telling me I should take real estate classes and that I would be great at it. I had no desire to pursue that. I was all about that stable pay check. My family depended on it. I ended up not taking the offer of my previous employer and took a month break from working in general to get my thoughts in order.

One morning I woke up and said okay, I will sign up. I started a part-time job at another automobile company while I took my real estate classes. When I got licensed, I decided to hang my license at a large, well-known brokerage with the train of thought that I would have plenty of support. After my first client closed on his home and I received my first commission check I quit the part-time job I had and focused full-time on my new career in real estate. It was the second best decision I have ever made in my life! As I did this, I had a thought, I remembered my dad's words about controlling my income. Funny, huh?

After working at a Century 21 office for about 18 months, I spoke to my partner about looking into making a move to another company because I was topped off at a split (pay structure) and I felt it was too low for all the effort and results I was making with little to no support. We interviewed with several companies, but then after talking things through, we decided to open up our own brokerage called 606 Brokers. We both had managing experience, I had tons of experience with marketing and lead gen. I said, "Let's do it!"

We teamed up with two other like-minded individuals and opened our doors to the public. While this was happening, my health continued to slowly get worse. I had more control at first. I made some changes to my eating habits and exercise, but it wasn't enough.

The year after we opened, one of our partners decided to go in a different direction and we decided to double down and put everything we had into the business. At this time, I was now entering stage 4 kidney disease and my diabetes was not in control as it should have been due to all of the time and effort I was putting in to build the business and service my own clients.

We continued to build the office and our brand, while helping our own clients make the American Dream of home ownership come true. It was tough, but I did not know how to give up. My desire for helping others, building my own company, and achieving financial freedom was at the forefront at this point. It should have been my health! I know that now.

Fast forward, several months later I was now entering the last stage of kidney disease. My kidneys were not functioning enough for me to even focus on reading a chapter in a book, let alone my business and family. My doctors decided it was time to put me on peritoneal dialysis. Basically, I was hooked up to a machine for 8-10 hours a day to replace the function of my kidneys. I did not let it stop me, I continued to build the brokerage, I even took several vacations and hauled my machine with me. I still tried to enjoy life as much as I could and work as hard as I could.

Don't get me wrong, every day I had some sort of pain, fatigue, foggy brain, etc. But I took the bad with the good and was determined to be successful and help us achieve our goals. I was put on the transplant list at Northwestern Memorial Hospital and waited for a little over four years. While all this was happening my time on dialysis was progressing, what was once 8 hours was now 12-13 hours a day. My day consisted of unplugging, going to the gym, servicing my clients, helping run the office, coming home to eat, and plugging back in. Not the best quality of life but I knew this was a bridge to something better. *¡Sí se puede!*

During all this my father passed away in late January of 2018; it was hard for all of us. Lots of changes were coming my way. 2018 was hard, but a blessing at the same time. Soon after my dad's passing, I received a call from Northwestern Medicine that they had found a match from a deceased donor for not just a kidney, but also a pancreas! As we continued to build the brokerage, purchase a building, and rehab the entire thing, I was getting prepped to go into major surgery to change my life forever. As I write this, I stop to remember how much support and love I had around me during all this.

After my surgery I woke up in what felt like a tubular space ship—I guess getting an MRI—and was in horrible pain with tubes down my throat and wires plugged in everywhere. After several days in ICU, they moved me to a room and after some recovery sent me home after being there for two weeks. Within less than 24 hours I was back in the ER screaming in pain—worse than before! They realized after some tests that the pancreas that had been transplanted into my body had pancreatitis. That led to a 10-11 week stay at the hospital, after several visits to ICU back and forth due to internal bleeding and other complications. The recovery I had to accomplish to be released was tough but I did it.

Eventually I was released and started to feel a little better. I didn't go back to work for 6-7 months as I had to heal from my surgical wounds. One thing I remember thinking to myself was how blessed I was to have this *gift*, because that is what my new organs were—a *gift!* Someone passed away and that individual's family decided to donate the organs and tissue to save so many lives. I am so grateful and blessed. As I slowly recovered and went back to the real estate world, Covid hit!

2020, wow, you already know. Here I am, still not 100%—what do I do? I did what I thought was best and was told. I stayed home… until I didn't! I noticed that my fellow colleagues were doing great. Against everyone's advice, I put on a mask and gloves and went out. I turned what was left of 2020 into the most successful year I have ever had at the time.

In nine months, I helped 51 individuals/families either sell or purchase their home. Keep in mind I was not 100%. I still had stuff coming out of my wounds and infections that I was cleaning in between my appointments, crazy right?! I didn't want to stop! Like I said I don't know how—well, I didn't. Now I do. As time went on, I healed and continued to build the office and purchased more property. As time passed my business grew.

One evening after attending an event on investing in Puerto Rico we decided to jump again and purchased a home in Puerto Rico to leverage as an Airbnb business. That has become a great success, and I plan to grow that business into several more Airbnb locations.

My immigrant parents chose to come here to build a better life for us and give my sister and I the opportunity to choose our paths. I don't know where I would be without their love and support. How they showed me the difference between working hard for a stable paycheck and working hard for yourself. One of my favorite books is *Rich Dad Poor Dad.* My father and mother were both. Funny how life is. Learn from your parents, ask them questions. I have so many I wish I would have asked my father before he passed. I now ask my mom questions all the time.

I am very excited to continue to build as I prioritize my health. I am not done building; this is only the beginning. I have several goals that I plan to achieve, but right now I'm putting my health first. I know it sounds like a cliche but it's so true, without good health nothing matters.

If you take anything from my story, I hope it's that you put your health first as you pursue anything in life. We all have obstacles; it's how we deal with them that matters. I am in a better place now and grateful to have the support of my family and friends that I care for dearly.

I would like to thank them for their unwavering support and I am so grateful for my parents that instilled the roots of having faith in our God and that anything is possible with hard work. I will be forever grateful.

TIPS FOR WEALTH & SUCCESS

- Take care of your health.
- Exercise at least three times a week.
- Ask questions everywhere you go. Stay curious.
- Find a mentor in what you are passionate about or what you want to follow as your business.
- Take leaps of faith; educate yourself before you jump, but JUMP!
- Try to live within your means and save money.
- Start your financial planning with a professional at an early age.
- Be open to change, change is good.
- Find out who you really are and own it! It's never too late.

BIOGRAPHY

Antonio Jose Sarmiento is a successful award-winning realtor, real estate investor, and co-owner of 606 Brokers, a Chicago based real estate brokerage. He was born and raised in Chicago. Son of immigrant hard working parents that came to the US from Barranquia, Colombia. He has a passion for helping people achieve financial wealth through real estate. He has helped hundreds of individuals and families. Antonio leads with confidence and a mindset to get things done.

Antonio also owns a successful Airbnb business in Aguadilla, Puerto Rico, and owns properties in Chicago with ongoing plans to own more vacation rentals.

He is a proud father of one, a son who is a Naval aviation mechanic. A loving brother to his sister Lissette and brother-in-law Doug, and son to his mother Humbelina Sarmiento. He has an unwavering faith in his God.

He is also a huge advocate for The Gift of Hope, an organization that helps promote organ donation and its importance as he is a post-transplant recipient himself.

He enjoys helping people with real estate and looks forward to what life has in store for him and his family.

Antonio Jose Sarmiento

Colombia

THE POWER OF CHANGE

ESTEFANIA ROA

"Success isn't about avoiding failure—it's about embracing the lessons, rewriting the narrative, and proving that no dream is out of reach."

I was born in Mexico, in a home filled with love, warmth, and rich traditions that shaped my early years. My grandparents raised me with care, providing stability despite economic hardships. My childhood was marked by afternoons playing in courtyards, the joy of family gatherings, and the stories my grandmother shared, instilling in me a deep sense of belonging.

Sundays at my grandmother's house were sacred—family would gather from all around, filling the home with laughter and joy as my grandmother devoted herself to the kitchen, ensuring everyone felt cared for and satisfied. The aroma of traditional dishes filled the air, and these moments became the foundation of my cultural identity. We celebrated Día de los Muertos, Posadas, had late nights at my uncles' ranch, and spent evenings listening to ghost stories about abandoned haciendas. This was the world I grew up in, rich in heritage and unity.

Yet, to my misfortune, early years were also marked by profound loss. My mother left me with my grandparents when I was just three years old, and for many years, I did not see her. The absence was deeply painful—I longed for her presence and imagined what it would be like to have a real family. I yearned for a sense of belonging, for a home that felt complete. At six years old, I was a victim of abuse—an experience that left deep scars and shaped my early perception of the world. This trauma made me feel disconnected, sending me on a desperate search for love and a place to call home.

As an adult, I carried the weight of that pain in ways I didn't fully understand at the time; It shaped my self-worth, making me believe I had to prove my value through perfection and overachievement. It affected my relationships, leading me to seek validation in places where love was conditional or unhealthy. For years, it fueled a battle within myself—between the fear of being vulnerable and the deep desire to be seen, heard, and understood. Healing is a journey, and I have learned that my past does not define me. My experiences have given me resilience, empathy, and a voice to advocate for others who have felt unseen. Today, I choose to break the cycle, to lead with strength, and to redefine what love, success, and self-worth truly mean.

CHILDHOOD CHALLENGES AND EARLY REJECTION

When I was eight years old, my life took a radical turn. My mother, whom I had barely known, decided to take me to the United States. The thought of reuniting with her filled me with anticipation, but also uncertainty. As I watched Mexico's landscape fade from the airplane window, I realized I was leaving behind everything familiar to step into an unknown world. As an eight-year-old girl, I was stepping into a country where I knew no one, believing that my mother would be my safety net and that we would finally be together. However, instead of comfort, I found myself facing a dark chapter that forced me to mature far beyond my years. I learned to accept this loneliness, and this shaped the way I approached close relationships throughout my life.

During this challenging time, the only solace I found was being close to my siblings as my mother was consumed by her addiction to alcohol. Her love was absent from my life and dealing with her illness at such a young age was incredibly painful. I endured the physical abuse, but the emotional and mental scars were even deeper. My childhood was not one of innocence or guidance—I had no one to talk to, no one to seek advice from. In this new country, I also faced a language barrier, cultural differences, and an emotionally unstable environment. Unlike the security I had known in Mexico, life here felt isolating. I longed for the warmth of my grandmother's home, but I had to adapt to my new reality.

Despite my home life, I pushed myself to do well in school. I worked hard to learn this new language and paid attention to the encouragement of teachers and others who told me I was intelligent and capable. Yet, I did not feel that way. Looking back now, I see how difficult it is for so many children to navigate the pressure of feeling inadequate and alone. I had no aspirations, no clear idea of what my future could hold. I had to trust that life has a way of connecting things over time, and even in my darkest moments, my journey was being shaped.

Family life was complicated. After another separation from my mother, our long-awaited reunion did not match my expectations. Instead of the love and connection I had hoped for, I was met with emotional distance. At twelve, I sought out my father in Mexico, only to experience another rejection—he denied his paternity. His family also rejected me, yet for years, I clung to the idea of being close to him. It took time to let go and realize that he was the one missing out on me—not the other way around.

BATTLES WITH ADVERSITY

After meeting my father and experiencing his rejection, I chose to stay in Mexico for a few more years, once again living with my grandparents. During this time, I attended secondary school, but I became rebellious as I was angry at the world, confused, and searching for something to fill the emptiness I carried inside. In that rebellion, I met someone who claimed to love me and desperate for affection, I believed him.

He became the father of my child. When I found out I was pregnant at the age of fourteen, it spread like a virus—an epidemic that no one wanted to be nearby for. Friends disappeared, opportunities vanished, and school became a distant memory. No one offered me guidance or support. It was as if my life had already been declared a failure before it had even begun.

At fifteen, I became a mother—an experience that transformed my life. My son's father was five years older than me, and without realizing it, I was repeating patterns of abuse, alcoholism, and deception. Although I was young and unprepared, my son became my anchor. He gave me purpose, and his well-being became my priority. Without a full education, the road ahead was challenging, but I was determined to provide a better life for him.

After separating from my son's father, the responsibility of raising my child fell entirely on me; I felt like I was repeating a cycle I did not know how to break. I made choices that harmed my well-being, seeking solace in self-destructive behaviors. Lacking a consistent parental figure and burdened by my past, I struggled to find stability. The loneliness and rejection I endured led me down difficult paths. I wanted a sense of purpose that would drive me toward change. I prayed for an opportunity—one that would allow me to create a life beyond the circumstances that had defined my past.

RESCUE AND TRANSFORMATION

In search of stability, I worked in various jobs, one of which was as a bank teller. This job gave me financial security and a newfound sense of direction. However, my life took another unexpected turn when my stepfather offered me the opportunity to rescue a bankrupt business. The company was drowning in debt, with no contracts in sight. Despite my lack of industry experience, I took the risk. The challenge was enormous—I faced multiple lawsuits, family conflict, and lost friendships—but every obstacle strengthened my resilience. Each time I hit rock bottom, I had to reinvent myself.

Three years ago, I faced one of my hardest trials—my business partner and I parted ways when I bought out his shares of the company. Soon after, I discovered that he had been involved in hidden conversations and secretive planning, supporting my own brother in starting a competing company in the same industry. Many around me were aware of these discussions except for me, and the layers of deception and unspoken truths made the situation even more painful. My brother joined in this effort, taking my best field employee with him and making him a business partner. This was a reality I had to accept—that everyone has the right to pursue their own path, that what I do is not exclusive to me, and that even my family could become my competition.

Despite the anguish and pain, I learned an invaluable lesson—to accept my place in people's lives without resentment or ego. Today, I am at peace and genuinely wish them success. My goal and success has never been about leading a company with over 30 employees, or rescuing a bankrupt business or mastering a complex industry. I view success in how many lives I can impact and inspire along the way, how many times I can share my story so that someone else can say, "If she could do it, so can I."

My success lies in the possibilities for this new generation, in looking into the eyes of those whom no one believed in and watching them persevere. Success, for me, was about breaking cycles, barriers, and being the black sheep of the family—the one who dares to challenge beliefs, stepping away from traditional paths that have frustrated entire generations. My success lies in detoxifying outdated mindsets and creating new family legacies.

SUCCESS AND LEADERSHIP

Over time, the business I initially took a risk on began to thrive. As a Latina woman in a male-dominated industry, I faced discrimination and skepticism. Yet, I persisted. Today, I am the only Latina woman in Illinois leading a structural steel coatings business. This achievement is a testament to the power of perseverance and the ability to transform adversity into opportunity. However, leadership is more than just a title—it is a responsibility. It means carrying the weight of decisions that impact not just my employees but their families and futures. It requires setting an example of integrity, resilience, and vision. Leadership demands constant learning, humility, and the ability to uplift others even when the. path is uncertain. I am still growing into the leader I aspire to be, as my dreams are still bigger than me, and my journey is far from over.

I continue to set new goals that challenge me beyond my current achievements. There are still barriers to break, ceilings to shatter, and stereotypes to dismantle. The construction industry remains an incredibly tough space for women, especially for a Latina like me as we have to prove ourselves twice as much. We need to work harder, and assert our place in an environment that was never designed with us in mind. Emerging as a leader in this field means pushing back against outdated mindsets, challenging long-standing norms, and opening doors for the next generation of women who will follow in my footsteps.

Through every challenge, I have learned that success is not about avoiding failure—it is about confronting it head-on. Growth requires risks, resilience, and the courage to keep going, even when the odds seem insurmountable. My faith has been my anchor through every storm, reminding me that I am never alone.

TIPS FOR SUCCESS & WEALTH

Business Advice for New Entrepreneurs:

Building a business is not about knowing everything from the start—it's about having the courage to take risks, adapt, and push forward even when the odds are against you. You may face financial hurdles, betrayals, self-doubt, or industry barriers, but every challenge is an opportunity to pivot, grow, and redefine success.

- **Bet on Yourself** – Experience is built along the way. Trust your ability to figure things out.
- **Lead with Integrity** – True success isn't just about profits; it's about the impact you make.
- **Stay Unshakable in Crisis** – Business will test you, but resilience will set you apart.
- **Break Cycles, Not Just Barriers** – Challenge outdated mindsets and create a lasting legacy.

Remember: "Your Greatest Strength is Resilience."

BIOGRAPHY

Estefania Roa embodies resilience, determination, and the power of transformation. Born in Mexico and raised in the U.S., she overcame abandonment, hardship, and the challenges of being a young mother at 15. Defying the odds, she became the owner and CEO of L.B. Hall Fireproofing, revitalizing a bankrupt company and leading it to success in a male-dominated industry.

A founding member of UNIDOS in Construction, Estefania advocates for equitable opportunities in the industry while supporting local communities. Passionate about empowering women, she founded the HOLA HAPPY Foundation, which provides mentorship, education, and career development for young single mothers, helping them break cycles of financial instability.

She is also a co-author of three book anthologies, using her story to inspire women facing adversity. Her influence has earned her numerous accolades, including Diversity Journal's Women Worth Watching, the 100 Women to Know in America list, and Construction Business Owner's Outstanding Women in Construction Award, among many others.

As a certified life coach, Estefania champions

emotional intelligence, faith, and strategic leadership. With her three children as her greatest motivation, she continues breaking barriers, mentoring future leaders, and proving that immigrants are not bound by their circumstances but by their ability to rise.

Her journey is a testament to perseverance, empowerment, and the belief that with faith, grit, and vision—anything is possible.

Estefania Roa
Mexico

ABOUT THE AUTHOR

Guillermo Chávez-Angeles

State Farm Agent | Entrepreneur | Real Estate Investor | Community Leader

Guillermo Chávez-Angeles actively lives out the motto, "The more good you put into the world, the more you get back." He brings his care and concern for the community into his daily role as a successful State Farm Agent, entrepreneur, real estate investor, and community leader. He finds great reward in helping provide customers the security and protection they need through State Farm insurance as he establishes long-term relationships with clients to grow together for a bright future.

Originally from Guadalajara, Jalisco, Mexico, Guillermo is deeply grateful to his parents for their sacrifices to provide a new life in the United States for himself and his three sisters. In 2001, he began his professional journey in the mortgage industry, where he helped individuals and families achieve homeownership for almost a decade. Guillermo's entrepreneurial spirit truly activated when the recession hit. Instead of succumbing to the challenge, he met it head-on, entering the real estate market to assist homebuyers in finding the solutions they needed.

However, in 2014, Guillermo embraced an opportunity to become an agent with State Farm, an established and respected brand with core values that resonated with his own. His business acumen led to his successful enterprise today, with a dedicated team of 12 associates across two locations (Elk Grove Village and Niles, Illinois). State Farm recognized his commitment to excellence and impact in the industry with their prestigious Chairman's Circle and Ambassador Travel recognitions for achievers in the top 10% of the company.

Guillermo gives back to his real estate and Hispanic community as a dedicated leader in the National Association of Hispanic Real Estate Professionals (NAHREP), the largest Latino business organization in the U.S. He served as President of the DuPage chapter in 2021. NAHREP focuses on educating, empowering, and closing the wealth gap through affordable homeownership within the Hispanic community and also promotes political action to ensure representation on the community level.

Guillermo's commitment to lifelong learning is key to his success in working with others and growing professionally. He is an avid reader of books by Miguel Ruiz, Darren Hardy, and Ed Mylett and a subscriber to self-development podcasts. His greatest joy comes from traveling and spending time with his family while knowing that his work makes a difference for the people he serves.

Made in the USA
Monee, IL
18 April 2025

15900897R00085